7 SIMPLE STEPS TO HEARING GOD'S VOICE

Listening to God Made Easy

SINDY NAGEL

Copyright © 2015 Sindy Nagel

All Rights Reserved

Copyright © 2015 Sindy Nagel. All rights reserved. No part of this book may be used or reproduced by any means, graphic, electronic, or mechanical, including photocopying, recording, taping, or by any information storage-retrieval system, without the written permission of the author, Sindy Nagel, except in the brief quotations embodied in critical articles and reviews. Do not sell this book in any form for personal gain.

All Scripture quotations, unless otherwise indicated, are taken from the Holy Bible, New International Version®. Copyright ©1973, 1978, 1984, 2011 by Biblica, Inc.™ Used by permission of Zondervan. All rights reserved worldwide. www.zondervan.com The "NIV" and "New International Version" are trademarks registered in the United States Patent and Trademark Office by Biblica, Inc.™

The NIV Bible does not capitalize the God pronouns. However, the author capitalized all God pronouns (i.e. He, His, Him, Himself, etc.) in all Bible verses and quotes listed in this book in order to give our awesome God the honor and glory He deserves.

Scripture quotations noted (NASB) taken from the New American Standard Bible®, Copyright ©1960, 1962, 1963, 1968, 1971, 1972, 1973, 1975, 1977, 1995 by The Lockman Foundation, Used by permission. (www.Lockman.org)

Paperback ISBN 978-0-9969934-0-1
eBook ISBN 978-0-9969934-7-0
Audio Book ISBN 978-0-9969934-3-2

Edited by Monique Bos

Cover Design by Angie Ayala and Rob at C5 Designs from www.fiverr.com

Cover Photo(s) by ©Valentyn_Volkov from www.depositphotos.com

7 Simple Steps to Hearing God's Voice – Infographic © Sindy Nagel. Stairs to the doors of heaven ©nicomenijes, Purchased Stock Image ID: 48106627 from www.depositphotos.com

7 Ways to Start Your Time with God – Infographic © Sindy Nagel. Designed by ©analuzsandrea from www.fiverr.com

7 Rewards of Hearing God's Voice – Infographic ©Sindy Nagel. Jewel illustration ©rea_molko, Purchased Stock Illustration Vector ID: 51251321 from www.depositphotos.com

This is absolutely the most wonderful book I have ever read, as Sindy skillfully and articulately describes how she learned the art of listening to God! With insight and wisdom, she instructs and encourages us to enter into that deeper relationship with Jesus Christ.—Ellen Neal, Director of Prayer and Inner Healing Prayer Ministries, Centerpoint Church, Kalamazoo, Michigan

Sindy's book is very encouraging! She not only reminds us that we can hear God's voice, Sindy also shares the listening techniques that can help us develop a more intimate relationship with the Lord. In her personal journal entries, she demonstrates her open heart and her transparency with God.— Carol D.

The many Bible verses that back up Sindy's words are very good. I particularly enjoyed how she reveals personal and private aspects of her story and describes the "how to" of listening to God.— Sue F.

Sindy Nagel's book will be a revelation of truth to many people, even many Christians! God, through His Holy Spirit, really does speak to us and desires a relationship through dialogue. Sindy's book explains in a straightforward way how to embark on the most magnificent human adventure—conversing with our God and Creator.—Craig Witcher, owner of Manna Café in Grand Rapids, Michigan, and founder of Manna Ministries Worldwide.

To honor and glorify the Father, Son and Holy Spirit; I do believe, I am listening, and I will obey. I'm an ordinary girl, listening to the Holy Spirit within me!—Anne K.

So many times when God spoke through Sindy in the book, it was as if He was speaking directly to me! I've been blessed.—Kathy H.

Is it possible God would speak to me? I had accepted Jesus as my Lord and Savior over thirty years ago but did nothing to learn His Word in the Bible. Reading Sindy's book affirmed that it was God's words I had heard. He loves me and desires that I spend time with Him in two-way conversation. He eagerly listens and will respond in a multitude of ways. If you like "How To" books, you'll love this one. Sindy describes how to converse with God and experience a closer relationship with Him. Thank you, Sindy.—Annette W.

As Sindy shares her personal experiences and biblical insights you will learn the discipline and art of turning a listening ear toward the heart of God and you will make a delightful discovery; God is longing to speak intimate, loving, and extraordinary things to YOU! As you learn to respond in two-way conversation with the Holy Spirit, your life will be forever changed.—Bethany C.

Sindy's book and Bible study have been life changing for me. As a new Christian, it has given me brand new insight as to the relationship I can have with my heavenly Father. I immensely appreciated Sindy's willingness to be honest and open about her journey as she learned to listen to God.—Kelly L.

I appreciated Sindy's honesty in sharing her personal journey to learning how much Jesus loves His children. The study was an inspiration to me.—Mary R.

Thank you, Sindy, for sharing your treasures with us. It was the best Bible study I have ever participated in. The timing couldn't have been any better.—Cindy B.

This book is dedicated to the One who stood at the door of my heart and knocked. He called to me, "Here I am!" He waited patiently for me to hear His voice and open the door. I am eternally grateful that He continued to speak to me until I heard and recognized His voice. My humble response is, "Speak, for your servant is listening!"

Acknowledgements

To my husband and children, thank you for your continuous encouragement and support in my writing and publishing endeavors. I appreciate the freedom you give me to spend large amounts of time on my passion for writing and sharing with the world the words God so generously gives me.

To my faithful family and friends who walk by my side offering me great ideas on how to improve the clarity and strength of my writing. Some of you are named here:

Amy	Jody	Rhiannon
Angie	Josh	Roxanne
Anne	Julie	Sally
Annette	Kathy	Sandy
Bethany	Kathryn	Sandra
Carol	Kelly	Sharry
Cindy	Linda	Shelly
Coree	Lori	Shirley
Craig	Marcia	Stephanie
Doug	Mary	Sue
Ellen	Midgie	Trish
Jenny	Nicole	Valerie
Jess	Renae	Valorie

Table of Contents

INTRODUCTION 1
   7 Simple Steps - Infographic 3
STEP 1 – EXPECT AND BELIEVE 5
   The Holy Trinity 8
   The Holy Spirit 10
STEP 2 – MAKE THE TIME 23
STEP 3 – ESCAPE THE CROWDS AND NOISE 37
   7 Ways to Start Your Time with God 45
   7 Ways to Start Your Time with God – Infographic 46
STEP 4 – WRITE IT DOWN 50
STEP 5 – PRACTICE DAILY 65
   Know God's Character 72
   Know the Character and Ways of Satan 74
   Discern What You Hear 82
STEP 6 – ENJOY THE REWARDS 89
   Absorb the Healing 91
   Find Freedom in Forgiveness 97
   Enjoy the Encouragement 100
   Follow the Instructions 108
   Consider the Conviction 118
   Savor the Wisdom 129
   Delight in the Peace 136
STEP 7 – SHARE THE GOOD NEWS 144
CONCLUSION 154

INTRODUCTION

God doesn't speak to me. Do you believe this? I confess, I did. Not once in twenty years of following Christ had I considered that God would speak to me, an average person. I knew He spoke to prophets, pastors, missionaries, and other spiritually mature individuals, but I never thought *I* could hear God's voice. However, one evening about fifteen years ago, it all changed for me. I heard a voice in my thoughts that I knew was not my own. It was God! He spoke to *me*, an average girl. Now I know ordinary people hear from God too. Are you ordinary? If you are, this book was written just for you.

You may wonder, *Will God speak to me? Does everyone hear God's voice? Does He speak to all people?* I myself wrestled with these same questions. In my quest for answers, God blessed me far beyond my heart's desire. My relationship with the Lord grew stronger and deeper as I learned how to enjoy two-way conversation with Him. Whenever we listen to God's voice within us, we achieve a greater intimacy with the Lord. Hearing God's voice is one of the *keys* to experiencing the abundant life Jesus Christ came to give us. The good news is…If you have accepted Jesus Christ as your Savior, God has already equipped you with everything you need to hear His voice.

God does speak to you! Are you listening to Him? Are you willing to try it? What have you got to lose?

You might be thinking, *I don't know how to listen to God's voice.* This book will answer your questions, walk you through a proven process to hearing from God, and refresh your spiritual connection with His Holy Spirit who dwells within you. Your unending search for how to recognize God's voice is over. After regularly hearing Him speak for the last fifteen years, I've developed a simple seven-step guide anyone can follow. The chapters of this book explain the ideas behind each of the seven steps. Applying these seven principles to your daily quiet time will strengthen and deepen your relationship with the Lord. Make Him first priority in your day, and seek to know Him better by listening to His voice within you. The rewards far outweigh the effort. Truly, it's time well spent!

Grab your free copy of the 7 Simple Steps color infographic .jpg file on the "Welcome!" page of my website:

www.sindynagel.com

STEP 1

EXPECT AND BELIEVE

My first mid-life depression brought me to my knees. I dwelled in a pit so deep only the long arm of the Lord could reach down and rescue me. God used the depression as a wakeup call for me. He got my attention so He could show me the depth of His great love for me and lead me into a more intimate relationship with Himself.

Prior to this period of spiritual awakening, God did not hold a prominent position in my demanding life. He never got the first few moments of my day; He fought for the leftovers—when I squeezed in time for Him. Had I known what I was missing, I would have fully embraced the idea of giving God first place in my life, before *everything* else. It wasn't until I fell into a dark abyss and questioned the reason for my existence that I needed God. I wondered, ***Is this all there is to life?*** If so, I wasn't sure I wanted to go on. Why did I feel so empty and alone when Jesus lived in my heart? Why didn't I experience a close relationship with my heavenly Father? How is intimacy with the God of the universe achieved? I soon learned the answers to these questions and more. Now I am excited to share my discoveries with you.

To achieve and maintain closeness with God, we must regularly draw near to Him. James 4:8 says, "Come near to God and He will come near to you." God loves us more than we will ever fully comprehend. He desires a close, personal relationship with each one of His children. However, He doesn't force Himself upon us. He passionately pursues us and patiently waits for our response. God chased after me for many years, but I didn't realize it. I didn't fully understand the love of God for me—until I learned to listen to His voice.

STEP 1 - EXPECT AND BELIEVE

To hear God's voice, we must *expect* and *believe* we will hear it. In faith, we should not doubt that God speaks to us. James 1:5-7 says,

> If any of you lacks wisdom, he should ask God, who gives generously to all without finding fault, and it will be given to him. But when he asks, he must believe and not doubt, because he who doubts is like a wave of the sea, blown and tossed by the wind. That man should not think he will receive anything from the Lord.

Doubt kept me from hearing God's voice for many, many years after I became a Christian. My skepticism resulted in a lack of spiritual intimacy with Jesus Christ for the first two decades of my life as a believer. I knew being a Christian meant enjoying a relationship with Jesus Christ. I thought I had one, but I didn't really consider that it required two-way conversation with Jesus to maintain that closeness. Unfairly, I talked to God, but I didn't pause to listen to His response. I never dreamed one of the voices in my head might be the Spirit of God within me.

In John 8:47, Jesus says, "He who belongs to God hears what God says." Jesus said it, so you can believe it! When you belong to God, you *will* hear Him. The next verse helped me when I found myself hesitating: "I do believe; help me overcome my unbelief!" (Mark 9:24). To hear God's voice, we must first *believe* we will hear it—believe, and then anticipate hearing it.

I attribute my years of doubt to a deficiency in knowing and understanding God. More precisely, I needed to better understand His Holy Spirit within me. It's absolutely vital we grasp the idea of who the Holy Spirit is in order to **expect** we will hear God's voice and **believe** God speaks to us. To better understand the Holy Spirit, we must first look at the Holy Trinity.

The Holy Trinity

The Holy Trinity is the most powerful, amazing relationship that ever existed. It's a profound mystery that the human mind will never completely understand. God in all three persons—Father, Son, and Holy Spirit—existed together from the beginning. Three unique beings operate as one God who is omnipotent, omniscient, and omnipresent.

When I say the word *God*, I use it interchangeably to speak about any one of the three, or all three at once. His math, 1+1+1=1, is different than our math, 1+1+1=3. We should not even try to define, or confine, Him with our understanding. It's important to know we have the ability to hear God speak because His Spirit lives within us. The Holy Spirit is God's voice in us.

We are able to communicate with all three members of the Godhead. They are three separate beings, and yet one God. I can speak to each of them individually or as one, interchangeably. When I speak to one, I know all three are listening. When one speaks to me, I know all three members of the Godhead join in on the conversation. It's like being on the telephone on a party line or a conference call with God, Jesus, and the Holy Spirit. Don't let this overwhelm you, and don't try to figure it all out. The main thing is you hear the voice of God. It doesn't matter whether it's the Father, Son, or Holy Spirit. It only matters that you know and understand that as a believer, you have the ability to hear God speak through the Holy Spirit within you.

The Holy Spirit

When Jesus died on the cross, He didn't stay in the grave, and He didn't leave us alone as orphans to fend for ourselves. He gave us a far greater gift—God raised Him from the dead, and He sent the Holy Spirit to live inside the heart of every believer. Did you hear that fantastic news? Jesus is alive, and the Holy Spirit is the *living* God who dwells in us and gives us life! We do not place enough value on this gift. It is priceless!

The moment we accept Jesus Christ as our Savior and Lord, God sends His Holy Spirit to live in us. By the Holy Spirit's power we are able to hear the voice of God within us, however it comes. The Holy Spirit never speaks of Himself, but reveals to us only what He knows and hears from God and Jesus. Also,

1. The Holy Spirit testifies about Jesus and glorifies Him. (See John 15:26, John 16:14)

2. The Holy Spirit testifies with our spirit that we are God's children. (See Romans 8:16)

STEP 1 - EXPECT AND BELIEVE

3. The Holy Spirit seals us as a deposit, guaranteeing our eternal inheritance until the day of redemption. (See Ephesians 1:13)

4. The Holy Spirit, our Counselor, counsels us in the wisdom of God. (See John 14:16)

5. The Holy Spirit, our Comforter, soothes us in times of sorrow, anxiety, and grief. (See 2 Corinthians 1:3-4)

6. The Holy Spirit, our Teacher, reminds us of what Jesus said and recalls Scripture to our minds. He properly interprets the Word of God for us. He teaches us the truth. (See John 14:26)

7. The Holy Spirit, the Spirit of truth, reveals the lies of the deceiver and replaces them with God's perfect truth from Scripture. He guides us into all truth. (See John 16:13)

8. The Holy Spirit, our lifeblood, lives within our spirit and ignites our faith. (See John 6:63, Ephesians 3:16-17)

9. The Holy Spirit empowers us to overflow with God's hope. (See Romans 15:13)

10. The Holy Spirit, through our spiritual conscience, teaches us right from wrong according to Scripture. He convicts us concerning sin, encouraging us to confess it and repent, or change our ways. (See John 16:8)

11. The Holy Spirit transforms us and encourages us to become exceedingly more Christ-like through the process of sanctification. (See 2 Thessalonians 2:13)

12. The Holy Spirit of Jesus, Immanuel, is God with us 24/7. (See Matthew 1:23)

13. The Holy Spirit communicates the voice of God from within us. He makes the things of God known to us. (See John 16:14)

14. The Holy Spirit gives us spiritual gifts from God. (See 1 Corinthians 12:4-11)

15. The Holy Spirit empowers us to do the will and work of God. (See Acts 1:8)

16. The Holy Spirit, our intercessor, helps us in our weakness. When we do not know what to pray, the Spirit prays for us in accordance with God's will. (See Romans 8:26-27)

The list goes on and on. Are you beginning to get the idea? The Holy Spirit of God indwelling us meets all our needs. Also, He connects us in relationship to God the Father and Jesus the Son. We know God better and experience more of Jesus through His Spirit within us. Watch for my forthcoming book, ***7 Roles of the Holy Spirit***, for a more in-depth study of some of the workings of the Holy Spirit.

The most astonishing part about all of this is the Holy Spirit is a *free gift* from God. Have you accepted this free gift? 1Corinthians 2:12 says, "We have not received the spirit of the world *but the Spirit who is from God*, that we may understand what God has *freely* given us" (emphasis mine). What a priceless gift it is indeed! Jesus took our place on the cross. All we have to do is invite Him into our hearts to be our Savior and Lord. When we do, both abundant life here on earth and eternal life with God in heaven are free for the taking. We can have the Spirit of the living God dwell in us without any cost to us. Truly, this is amazing grace!

If you do not accept Jesus as your Savior and invite Him to be the Lord of your life, you live apart from God now and for all eternity. The Bible clearly states, "God has given us eternal life, and this life is in His Son. He who has the Son has life; he who does not have the Son of God does not have life" (1 John 5:11-12). Life is difficult enough. Life without God is really no life at all. Claim Jesus as your Savior and Lord today! Experience all God planned for you in this life, and guarantee your inheritance of eternal life in heaven with Him.

I claim Ephesians 3:16-17 for you: "I pray that out of His glorious riches He may strengthen you with power through His Spirit in your inner being, so that Christ may dwell in your hearts through faith." Further evidence of the indwelling Holy Spirit is found in 1 John 3:23-24, "And this is His command: to believe in the name of His Son, Jesus Christ, and to love one another as He commanded us. Those who obey His commands live in Him, and He in them. And this is how we know that He lives in us: *We know it by the Spirit He*

STEP 1 - EXPECT AND BELIEVE

gave us" (emphasis mine). Likewise, Ephesians 1:13-14 tells us that God gave us the Spirit as a deposit, guaranteeing our eternal life in heaven. Not only does the Spirit enhance and empower our life on earth, He guarantees our entrance into heaven.

In John 16:13-15, Jesus says,

> But when He, the Spirit of truth, comes, He will guide you into all truth. He will not speak on His own; He *will speak* only what He hears, and He *will tell you* what is yet to come. He will bring glory to Me by taking from what is Mine and *making it known to you.* All that belongs to the Father is Mine. That is why I said the Spirit will take from what is Mine and make it known to you (emphasis mine).

This passage summarizes the main role of the Holy Spirit in how God speaks to His children. By the power of the Holy Spirit, we can hear God's voice, because His gift is God's Spirit in us. Does that resonate with you? I had heard many times that the Holy Spirit lives in me, but I had to think about it on a deeper level before I appreciated all this means and all He does for me. Consider Paul's prayer in Ephesians 1:17-20:

> I keep asking that the God of our Lord Jesus Christ, the glorious Father, may give you the Spirit of wisdom and revelation, so that you may know Him better. I pray also that the eyes of your heart may be

> enlightened in order that you may know the hope to which He has called you, the riches of His glorious inheritance in the saints, and His incomparably great power for us who believe. That power is like the working of His mighty strength, which He exerted in Christ when He raised Him from the dead and seated Him at His right hand in the heavenly realms.

Even more incredible than God living in us is that He gives us "His incomparably great power." You and I have the same power that raised Jesus from the dead! This concept is as inconceivable as the relationship of the Trinity. It's incredible and mindboggling. We can do all things in the power of the Holy Spirit of God who lives in us! Amen and Amen!

Knowing that God's Spirit lives in us helps us believe the Spirit of God speaks to us, not just occasionally, but all day, every day. We can hear the voice and will of God in everything we do, if only we listen. The Spirit makes things known to us, if only we pay attention. The Spirit comforts us, if only we receive it. The Spirit counsels us, if only we listen. The Spirit guides us, if only we ask. The Spirit teaches us, if only we become students of God. The Spirit protects us, if only we equip ourselves with the sword of the Spirit, which is the Word of God.

STEP 1 - EXPECT AND BELIEVE

Sometimes we don't recognize God's voice as distinct from ours because the Holy Spirit lives inside us, and our own spirits are so closely intertwined with God's that when we have thoughts, we just write them off as our own. We don't consider the Spirit of God might be speaking to us in our thoughts. I can't tell you how many times, and for how many years, I must have been hearing God's voice and didn't even know it.

How does the Holy Spirit make things known to us? He does it in at least four ways:

1. He guides our thoughts.
2. He speaks to us in our thoughts.
3. He prompts us in our spirit to do the things of God.
4. He speaks to us through God's Word, making it come alive with meaning for us.

In order to hear what the Holy Spirit tells us, we must *recognize* His voice within us. I have worked in office environments for more than thirty years. Most of that time, I worked in small offices where my responsibilities included answering the phone. After speaking to the same people day after day, my brain began to recognize the voice of each person I spoke with before the caller identified himself or herself. As soon as I answered a call and heard the voice on the other end, my mind ran the voice through my repertoire, and I determined the caller's identity without asking. Each person had a slightly different volume, tone, or inflection, as well as a unique manner of speaking. I also knew nearly everyone I spoke with, so I could put a face with the voice I heard, which made the calls more personal. I learned to recognize each caller's voice because I knew the person, and I had spoken with him or her many times before.

To recognize God's voice, we must get to know Him better and spend a lot of time listening to His voice. In John 10, Jesus, the Good Shepherd, says,

- ❖ "the sheep listen to His voice" (verse 3).
- ❖ "His sheep follow Him because they know His voice" (verse 4).
- ❖ "My sheep know Me" (verse 14).

We must spend time in God's Word, reading who He is, how He acts, the things He says and does, the character He has. You can

STEP 1 - EXPECT AND BELIEVE

go to virtually any book or chapter in the Bible and see who God is and how He speaks to His people. Understanding who He is and how He works in our lives will enable us to recognize His voice when we hear it in our thoughts. Spend time in God's Word and let it resonate with you. Discover who God is to you and ponder what He might say and how He might sound if He were to speak to you.

We have the *living* God inside us, so why wouldn't we be able to hear His voice? Some things may prevent us: doubt, fear, pride, worry, busyness, disobedience, and unwillingness to forgive, for example. To be clear, these behaviors won't necessarily keep God from speaking to us, but they may make us deaf to His voice. Learn more about each of these obstacles in my forthcoming book, *7 Roadblocks to Hearing God Speak*.

Practicing any or all of the seven behaviors above may cause you to feel the All-Powerful God won't speak to you because you're not worthy to hear Him. Truly, despite your flaws and feelings of inadequacy, God continues to pursue you passionately. He doesn't wait until you are perfect and sin-free to speak to you. If that were the case, none of us would ever hear from Him. Instead, the Holy

Spirit helps you become more Christ-like, so it's imperative you know how to hear and recognize His voice to utilize the promptings and assistance He offers you in the journey of sanctification. Ironically, listening to the Holy Spirit and hearing from God are vital for identifying and changing or eliminating the seven behaviors causing your deafness to Him.

One of the roadblocks to hearing God's voice is *lack of time* or busyness. The next step to hearing God's voice is making Him your first priority and meeting with Him daily. This practice greatly increases your ability to hear Him speak. Expect to hear His voice. **God does speak to you.** Believe the truth. **God desires an intimate relationship with you through two-way conversation.** Now, make time for Him.

STEP 1 - SELF-REFLECTION:

1. Are you a believer? Have you accepted Jesus as your Savior and invited Him into your heart to be your Lord? When did you do this?

2. Do you understand the role of the Holy Spirit? List one or two things that stood out to you from what you just read about Him.

3. Do you believe God will speak to you? If not, identify why.

4. If you already hear God's voice, how does it sound to you?

5. Which of the *7 Roadblocks to Hearing God Speak* do you relate to? List all that apply.

6. What other things keep you from hearing God speak?

7. Is *lack of time* one of the roadblocks preventing you from hearing God's voice? Why?

7-DAY CHALLENGE:

Over the next seven days, choose a different verse each day from the sixteen verses listed in "The Holy Spirit" section above. Look up the verse in your Bible and meditate on it. Ask God to reveal to you the truth about the Holy Spirit. Pay close attention to the thoughts God gives you as He speaks to your heart through the Scripture passage you read.

STEP 2

MAKE THE TIME

God wants you to hear this today: Despite how you feel and what you might believe, He loves you more than you know, and He wants to spend time with you. He wants you to put Him first in your life and listen to His voice. The first commandment God gave us in Deuteronomy 5:7 is, "You shall have no other gods before Me." Anything that keeps you from spending time with Him is another god. Anything you put more value on than your relationship with Jesus Christ is another god.

Deuteronomy 6:5 says, "Love the Lord your God with all your heart and with all your soul and with all your strength." God wants to be in first place in our lives. Don't be like me and wait until you are in dire straits to deepen your relationship with Jesus. Pursue Him now—seek Him with all your heart; and you will find Him. Remember? James 4:8 says, "Come near to God, and He will come near to you." God patiently waits for us to spend time with Him.

When I wanted to put God first in my life, I had to *make* time for Him. Can you relate? I worked full time, raised a family, chauffeured my children to sports and other activities, and participated in Bible studies and church ministries. I did all the right things and I followed Jesus, but still my heart suffered a hollow sense. Discontent and dissatisfaction bred my search for more. *This could not be all God planned for me.* I soon realized I hadn't left any time to be alone with God and just listen to Him.

My Christian mentor, who had been listening to God speak, encouraged me to find a quiet place where I could talk to God, and then be still and listen for His voice. First, I had to expect and believe. Next, I had to make the time. So I put God first by getting up earlier than my normal time every day. For me that meant instead of setting the alarm clock for 5:30 a.m., I had to set it for 5 a.m. or earlier. I started out with fifteen or twenty minutes, and as I spent time with God, I hungered for more and more of Him. The time grew into forty minutes, then sixty minutes and longer, because as I heard from God, I loved being with Him. I used this time just to "be in relationship" with Jesus Christ. I wanted to get to know God better. I wanted Him to grow me into the woman He had in mind when He created me.

At first, when I quietly sat with the Lord, it did not go completely well. I didn't know how to hear His voice. I got so bored in the silence that I fell asleep. So I had to figure out how to keep myself awake. I took a shower and let my cool, wet hair hang on my neck to keep myself from dozing off. I did not snuggle under a warm throw blanket or cover my cold feet with cozy slippers. Instead, I purposely made myself less than comfortable so I could be on full alert to hear my Savior's voice. Most importantly, I didn't quit when I did not hear God's voice right away. To hear Him speak requires patience on our part. How patient are we at listening for God's voice? Do we give up too easily if we don't hear Him immediately? Do we give up after five minutes of silence? Ten? Thirty? The key to hearing God speak is perseverance. As I made it a daily practice,

God honored my time, and eventually I heard and recognized His voice.

Even if you are not a morning person, meet with God for at least a few minutes at the beginning of each day to ask for His direction, and *listen* to what He says. You may hear something important before you start your day. Then actively listen and be aware of God's voice at unexpected times throughout the day. The Holy Spirit speaks to us all day long; however, we get distracted and forget to listen.

Determine your best time of day, the time when you function at your highest level, and block out a chunk of time for God. Carve out fifteen minutes to be with Him—just listening to His voice and writing down your conversation. Do you have a thirty-minute lunch? Why not spend it with God? Do you drive your children to a music lesson or sports practice? Talk to God while you wait for them. Do you spend a lot of time driving for your job? God will meet with you in your vehicle. Are you a night owl? Spend time with God after your family is in bed. Would you be willing to lose sleep in order to hear the voice of God? Watch for my future book, *7 Times to Listen*

to God, where I will explore in greater depth how to make time for Him.

If you don't hear from God right away, don't quit! He doesn't stop talking to you just because you don't hear Him the first time. Remember the story of Samuel (1 Samuel 3)? God called Samuel three times before Eli, the priest, realized it was God calling. He continues to pursue you until you hear Him. He pursued me for nearly two decades before He finally got my attention. When He did, my life quickly transformed from boring to amazing! We had a lot of lost time to make up for. So I spent hours in God's Word getting to know Him better and listening to His voice. We spoke at length on many occasions.

One of the shortest sentences in the Bible, 1 John 4:16, best describes His character: "God is love." If He is love, that means He'll speak to you in a loving way, with a loving tone and a message that comes from the depth of His love for you. In 1 Corinthians 13:4-8, Paul describes love in this way: "Love is patient, love is kind. It does not envy, it does not boast, it is not proud. It is not rude, it is not self-seeking, it is not easily angered, it keeps no record of wrongs. Love does not delight in evil but rejoices with the truth. It always protects, always trusts, always hopes, always perseveres. Love never fails."

If God is love, we can put His name in place of the word "love" in that passage: God is patient, God is kind. He does not envy, He does not boast, He is not proud. He is not rude, He is not self-seeking, He is not easily angered, He keeps no record of wrongs. God does not delight in evil but rejoices with the truth. He always protects, always trusts, always hopes, always perseveres. God never fails.

What a great picture of the character of God. When you are in conversation with Him, He will show you patience; He will be kind, not rude. He will not get angry easily. Once you have confessed and repented of your sins, He will keep no record of your wrongs. He does not delight in evil but rejoices with the truth. God will protect you, trust in you, give you hope, and persevere with you. He will never fail you. Isn't that worth your time?

In Exodus 34:6-7, God described Himself in this way: "The Lord, the Lord, the compassionate and gracious God, slow to anger, abounding in love and faithfulness, maintaining love to thousands, and forgiving wickedness, rebellion, and sin." God will speak to you with compassion. God will be gracious to you as He communicates with you. God will be slow to anger when you confess your sins and shortcomings to Him. God will abound in love and faithfulness toward you as you meet with Him. God will forgive your wickedness, rebellion, and sin. God will love you unconditionally and completely. That alone is worth your time.

Often we are afraid to communicate with God because of what we have experienced in communicating with our fellow human beings, especially authority figures in our lives. We expect God to treat us the way we have been treated by others, when in fact Jesus modeled how God acts toward us and how we should regard others. Since I have spent more time with God, the relationship I have experienced with Him has been quite different—exponentially better—than the expectations I originally had.

Consider your relationship with a best friend, a beloved child, or a loving parent. You don't do all the talking and then rush away from the conversation when you've said what you need to say.

You take turns talking and listening, asking and sharing. Your give-and-take conversation builds and strengthens the relationship. You can have that same kind of two-way communication with the Creator of the universe—He's waiting for you to join Him!

When I converse with God, He is very patient with me. I ask Him the same things over and over again, and He never grows weary of listening to me. He tirelessly repeats Himself and confirms what He has previously said to me. Sometimes He expands on the topic and reassures me of His love for me and His confidence in me. I can't believe the amount of patience God exercises with me. I don't get that from anyone else I speak with. He never makes me feel like I'm wasting His time or boring Him. God is committed to me, and He expects the same in return. That's why I obediently make time for two-way communication with God.

God is kind to me. God treats me with respect as He listens to me. He is never condescending. He doesn't make me feel insignificant or stupid. He greets me with excitement whenever I make time to be with Him. God is truthful. He never acts false or fake with me. He speaks the truth in love, telling me difficult things at times, but He does so in a loving, caring manner. God is so good to me, I eagerly make time for two-way communication with Him.

Most often when God speaks to me, His words bless me and convict me at the same time. God tells me what He sees in me, what I mean to him, and what He does for me, as well as how I could be doing better in areas important to Him. God speaks to me in love with words of encouragement that uplift me, along with words of inspiration that motivate me to act on the Holy Spirit's promptings. The direction I receive benefits me greatly.

God does not laugh at me, mock me, degrade me, or humiliate me, as a human audience might do. God listens to every word I say and eagerly responds with love, respect, devotion, and commitment. I verbalize my most intimate thoughts with the God of the universe, and He never talks down to me. I can be vulnerable and transparent with God because He already knows my every thought, deed, and emotion from the beginning of my life through eternity. God knows me better than I know myself, so He gives me insight into myself and my life.

I can go to God with a list, and He is patient while we cover each item. He lovingly encourages me in every thought or situation I bring before Him. God imparts His wisdom when I ask for it. He comforts me and uplifts me when I feel sad or depressed. He calms my spirit when I feel angry. He gives me peace when I experience turmoil. He builds me up when I am weak and weary. He counsels me when I need support. He leads me when I need guidance. He walks with me when I need a friend.

Now that I know God better and speak to Him often, I can't imagine life without Him. How did I ever get by before? That's exactly it. I just *got by* before. Now, my life is significantly more meaningful. God had a purpose for creating me, and being able to communicate with Him has completely changed the way I do life. In my humanness, I still forget to go to God first with everything, and I try to do things on my own. It's during the times I *do* go to God first that my life works out much better. Making time to participate in two-way communication with God is not only life-giving; it's lifesaving.

STEP 2 – MAKE THE TIME

Life is much more gratifying when I live according to God's plans than when I follow my own plans. I tend to get too busy when I run ahead on my own. I go in a different direction than the one God planned for me; I tie up my time with different activities than the ones He has in mind for me. God desires close relationship with His children. He would love to be in continual, all-day conversation with us. So I diligently try to make time for two-way communication with God.

When we believe in God and obey His commands, we have access to the power of God's Spirit within us. Satan will do everything in His power to make us so busy we don't have time to develop our relationship with Jesus Christ. Be intentional about making time for God—not because you should, but because your life will be much more fulfilling and peaceful when you are in tune with Him. When you do spend time with God, be sure to leave openings in the conversation for Him to speak. Don't do all the talking. Allow Him to say what's on His heart while you practice good listening skills. It will be the best part of your day.

I invite you and encourage you to put God first in your life. Make time to meet with Him alone and build a relationship with Him by listening to His voice. You may need to let something go. If you are not currently in an intimate relationship with Jesus Christ, I encourage you to set aside some of the things you are doing and make time for Him. Be alone with God, just listening to His voice. Don't let Satan shame you into giving it up altogether if you can't spend twenty or thirty minutes with God every day. God will take whatever time you give Him. He just wants to spend time with you and show you how much He loves you.

Now I'm an empty-nester, so I better understand how God feels toward us. My children both attend college an hour away and often don't find time to come home. After two or three weeks of not seeing them, I go through withdrawal. So I'm willing to drive two hours round trip to spend one hour with them at dinner. I assume they have to eat, right? So they can take an hour to eat while spending time with me. After all, I'm paying for their meal. I want to spend time with my children to catch up on their lives and to show them how much I love and care about them. I want to help guide them and give them my wisdom. I try to encourage them and build them up.

That's how God feels about us. He'll go to great lengths to be with us, and He'll take whatever amount of time we make for Him, just to show us how much He loves us and cares about us. While reading devotions, completing Bible studies, and reading God's Word are all practices of great value and importance, I pray you will also make time solely for listening to and conversing with God. When you persevere, practice listening, and wait on God, you will hear Him. Make time for God and find a way to escape the crowds and noise around you. It will be the best use of your time all day!

STEP 2 - SELF-REFLECTION:

1. Is God your first priority in life? If not, what needs to change to make that happen?

2. Do you ever make time to listen to God? If so, when?

3. During what part of your day could you carve out 15-20 minutes to converse with God?

4. In your conversations with others, are you a good listener? Identify one change you could make to become a better listener.

5. When you communicate with God, do you do all the talking, or do you give Him time to speak to you?

6. How long will you patiently wait to hear from God? Set a timeframe in your mind—5 minutes, 15 minutes, 20 minutes, or longer? Make it part of your listening practice.

7. How would hearing from God transform your life?

7-DAY CHALLENGE:

Make time three days this week, for fifteen minutes each day, to communicate with God in two-way conversation. Ask Him to tell you who you are in His eyes. Record what you hear.

STEP 3

ESCAPE THE CROWDS AND NOISE

As I age, every year I lose more of my ability to hear. Background noise is the worst. When I'm in a crowd, or there's a fan blowing or a radio playing, my hearing ability is greatly reduced by the extra noise. I blame my hearing loss on heredity and forty-some years of daily blow-drying my hair. Every morning I wash my hair and blow-dry it for five to ten minutes. Had I been smart many years ago, I would have worn earplugs to protect my hearing. But now, there is no way of getting back the hearing I've lost. My best chance of hearing someone well is to be alone with them, one on one, away from the noise of a crowd.

Likewise, my best chance of hearing God speak to me is to be alone with Him, one on one, away from the noise of a crowd. I encourage you to make a regular practice of sitting still in a quiet place, shutting out the world's noise, and listening attentively to the voice of God. Consider this verse from Psalm 62:1: "My soul waits in silence for God only; from Him is my salvation" (NASB).

1 Samuel 3 provides many examples of how to listen to God, and adopting a childlike attitude is one of the most important. Samuel's mother dedicated him to serving and worshipping the Lord. Even in his younger years, God spoke to him. This happened during a time when God rarely spoke to anyone, yet He chose to speak to a child. The idea that God holds a special place in His heart for children should cause us to wonder, *Why?*

Listed below are seven traits God loves in children:

1. An infant completely depends on his caregiver. Likewise, God wants us to depend on Him for everything. A child trusts wholeheartedly. God asks us to trust in Him with all our hearts.
2. A child's mind is open, receptive to new ideas.

3. A child's faith has not been tarnished by life's trials and disappointments.
4. A child waits with excitement and anticipation to see what will happen next.
5. A child comes before God with a pure heart, unburdened by responsibilities, regrets, fears, and doubts.
6. A child believes easily and expects to experience the goodness of God.
7. A child's mind remains in its own little world, not distracted by crowds and noise.

When did God choose to speak to Samuel? What posture did Samuel assume? God spoke to Samuel when he lay down at night. Samuel stilled himself before the Lord; he heard the voice of God because he remained in a quiet place with no noise or distractions. Also note Samuel and even Eli, the priest of God, did not recognize or realize right away it was God speaking to Samuel. God did not give up after the first try, however. He pursued Samuel again. In fact, He called Samuel three times before Eli understood. Our God does not give up on us if we don't hear Him the first time He speaks to us. Persistently, He speaks until we hear Him. Shouldn't we give

God as much in return by waiting expectantly to hear His voice? Shouldn't we give Him our full attention, away from people and commotion?

When Samuel did realize God spoke, he positioned himself to hear God again; he returned to a quiet place and remained still. He waited patiently. Then God called him again, and Samuel humbly said, "Speak, for your servant is listening." God spoke to him then, and He continued to appear at Shiloh and speak to him for many years, not letting His words fall to the ground or go unheard. He revealed Himself to Samuel through His word and His voice, and Samuel spread God's message to all of Israel.

We can take lessons from the boy Samuel on how to position ourselves to hear from God. Do you practice being still, in quiet solitude, expectantly and patiently waiting to hear God speak? When you do, you will hear the voice of God.

Jesus served as a great role model for how to have a relationship with the Father. As He became better known in His ministry, multitudes of people followed Him. In order to hear instructions and receive refreshment from God, Jesus escaped the

STEP 3 – ESCAPE THE CROWDS AND NOISE

crowds and found quiet places to be alone with His heavenly Father. Jesus had the Spirit of the Lord within Him, just as we do, but He still preferred to listen to the voice of God the Father away from the noise of the multitudes. He even separated Himself from His closest companions, His disciples, in order to pray and to hear God's voice: "Then Jesus went with His disciples to a place called Gethsemane, and He said to them, 'Sit here while I go over there and pray'" (Matthew 26:36).

As I decided to know God better and develop an intimacy with Christ, I eagerly got up early every morning to enjoy a quiet time with God. I used this time to journal my thoughts and prayers to Christ. I poured out my heart to Him. I shared my emotions, my fears, my joys, my anger, my desires—my most intimate feelings—with God. Then I tried to "be still, and know that He is God" (see Psalm 46:10).

I pictured Jesus sitting in my living room with me. He became a father, a husband, a friend, and a counselor all wrapped up into one. He knew my every need, even before I asked. I listened for His voice and direction in my life. When I spent time alone with God and heard His voice, I hungered for more time in conversation with Him. In Luke 6:21, Jesus says, "Blessed are you who hunger now, for you will be satisfied." Only God can satisfy the hunger in my soul; only He can fill that need.

I love early mornings. I function best in the morning, and I love watching the earth wake up. The birds begin singing before the first light of day. The wind gently whispers, blowing the leaves on the stoic trees. The bright morning sun peeks over the horizon before making its ascent. The rumble of loud trucks does not yet disturb the silence. Few people move about the neighborhood. My own household stays asleep. It's a time of solitude, peace, and tranquility. Early morning offers me the quietest time and the best chance of hearing God's voice. My mind is clearest first thing in the morning before I start thinking about all I have to do that day. I have made it my practice to get out of bed thirty to sixty minutes early to enjoy time with God away from the crowds and noise, even in the privacy of my own home. I completely relate to Psalm 5:3: "Morning by morning, O Lord, you hear my voice; morning by morning I lay my requests before you and wait in expectation."

I make some coffee and take my favorite spot on the living room sofa. I know this time belongs to God. I greet Him with a "Good morning, Lord" and begin my two-way conversation with the God of the universe. Sound simple? It has not always been so. When I first began my early morning practice of meeting with God, I felt unproductive. As I've said, often I fell asleep in the silence. Do you recall Jesus' frustration with His best friends who fell asleep when He had asked them to keep watch while He prayed? I don't want to be the one to fall asleep while meeting with the King of kings, do you? If not, do whatever it takes to stay awake and hear what God has to say to you.

Frequently, I found my mind wandering to the other noises in my head. When I became aware these things kept me from my purpose, I dealt with the distractions by writing them down. On a piece of paper, separate from my journal, I wrote down the busy thoughts that took up space in my mind and set them aside so I wouldn't forget about them later. Then I resumed my still, expectant state of waiting on God.

Now I begin my God time with a topic for the day, or I ask Him to give me a topic on which I meditate. As I start writing my own thoughts, my pen just keeps going, and I keep writing all the thoughts entering my mind. So many times I can go back and read what I wrote and distinguish where I stopped and where God started in my thoughts.

If you're not already in the practice of listening to God's voice, you may not know how to begin. I like variety, so I start my time with God in different ways each day. Below I share a few with you. If you have your own way already, don't change it. But if you are looking for new ways to spend time with God, try one of my *7 Ways to Start Your Time with God* as shown on the next page:

7 Ways to Start Your Time with God

1. Pick a passage from the Bible, or allow the Holy Spirit to lead you to a passage of Scripture, and meditate on it. Ask God to speak to you about the verses and how they relate to you. Listen for His voice from within you. Record what you hear Him say.

2. Begin a conversation with God by bringing your concerns or questions to Him. Allow Him to answer you in the moment. Many times, God wants to speak to us immediately. We don't always have to wait for His answers.

3. Ask God to speak to you about a trial or challenge you face, and allow Him to walk you through it and show you His presence.

4. Ask God to reveal the truth about who you are in His eyes. Write down what He says.

5. Ask God to describe His character and who He is to you.

6. Let God heal an emotional wound in your mind and heart. His encouraging, truthful words will restore your soul.

7. Ask God to set you free from the enemy's lies with His perfect truth. (For example, you might believe, "I am not enough.") Let God set you straight. Confirm it with His Word in the Bible, and memorize verses representing the truth.

7 Ways to Start Your Time with God

1. Meditate on Scripture asking God what He wants you to learn from it.
2. Bring a concern or question to God and wait for His reply.
3. Ask God to talk to you and walk you through a challenge or trial.
4. Ask God to reveal the truth about who you are in His eyes.
5. Ask God to describe His character and who He is to you.
6. Let God heal an emotional wound in your mind and heart.
7. Ask God to set you free from the enemy's lies with His truth.

Sindy Nagel©

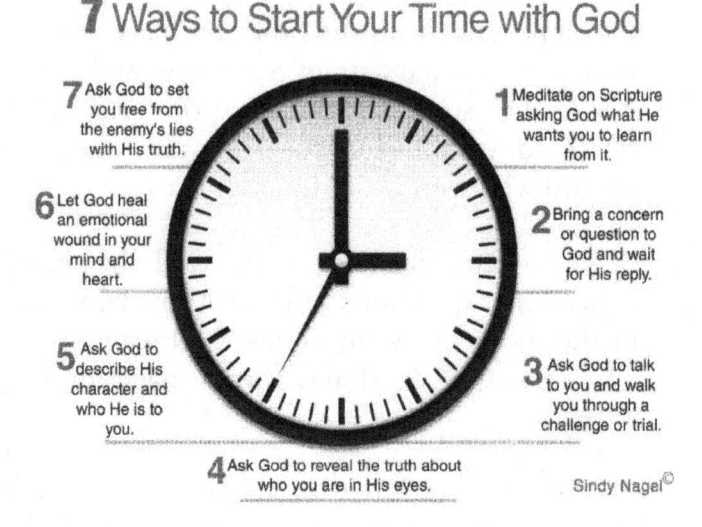

Watch for my forthcoming book, *7 Ways to Listen to God*, where I will describe methods and approaches to listening to God.

Be cautious not to put God in a box. There's not just one right way, one right time, or one right place to meet with Him. He will meet with you anywhere you are, any time of the day or night. You do not have to be in a prayer mode with your eyes closed to speak with and listen to God. He will speak to you

STEP 3 – ESCAPE THE CROWDS AND NOISE

wherever and whenever He has your attention. Sometimes I hear from God while I take a shower. Although a bit strange, it makes sense. I'm alone with the peaceful, soothing sound of running water, and He has my undivided attention, right?

Of course, you can communicate with Him in the middle of a noisy crowd, but don't make that your regular practice. He more often desires to meet with you one on one in a quiet place. Finding the time and place to meet with God alone may be your greatest challenge in life. Are you up for it? If you let him, God will help you rearrange your schedule. If you ask Him, God will present you with places and opportunities to be alone with Him. Make God your first priority and seek out a quiet place of solitude and rest. Watch for my forthcoming book, *7 **Places to Listen to God***, where I will communicate more ideas for escaping crowds and noise.

Ask a good friend to pray for you and hold you accountable to your goal as you seek to hear and discern God's voice. Have your friend pray these seven things:

1. You'll find a time and place to meet with God alone.
2. You'll be able to quiet your mind enough to hear Him, and your heart will be open to receiving God's voice however it comes to you.

3. God will speak to you, and you will clearly hear His voice.
4. All barriers preventing you from hearing God's voice will be broken, and God will protect you from the confusion and influence of the enemy.
5. Your relationship with Christ will grow deeper and stronger.
6. You'll absolutely love meeting with God, and it won't be a chore for you.
7. God will work with you, during this time, to bring you to the fullness of the creation He had in mind when He gave you the breath of life.

If you are not in an intimate relationship with Christ right now, I encourage you to set aside at least one thing on your busy schedule to make time for God and escape the crowds and the noise. Take a few minutes every day to be still and know God more intimately. Listen to His voice, hear what He says to you, and write it down. You'll be really glad you did!

STEP 3 - SELF-REFLECTION:

1. Which of the seven traits of children do you most relate to?

2. Which of those traits could you improve on?

3. How did Jesus escape the crowds and noise to listen to His Father?

STEP 3 – ESCAPE THE CROWDS AND NOISE

4. If you were to picture Jesus sitting with you, what do you see? Describe it. Next time you meet with God, use your description to picture Jesus sitting with you.

5. Which of the *7 Ways to Start Your Time with God* appeals to you? Identify it, and try it next time you meet with God.

6. Who could you ask to pray for you and hold you accountable to listening to God?

7. What challenge or concern would you most like to receive God's wisdom for? Make that the topic of your next conversation with God.

7-DAY CHALLENGE:

This week, find a new place to meet with God away from people, noise, and distractions. Choose one of the **7 Ways to Start Your Time with God** and spend twenty to thirty minutes talking and listening to God.

STEP 4

WRITE IT DOWN

The best advice my Christian mentor offered me about listening to God's voice was, "Write it down." The older I get, the more I have made myself dependent on writing notes to remind myself to do something. Writing down an idea reinforces it in my mind, so I will more accurately remember it later. The practice of writing in a journal absolutely, unequivocally produced for me the desired success in hearing the voice of God and maintaining the integrity of His words. Additionally, journaling your conversations with God offers many excellent benefits.

Most importantly, recording your communication with the Holy Spirit affords you the opportunity to differentiate your thoughts from God's thoughts. Secondly, you can return to your journaled conversations with the Lord when you experience times of disconnect from Him. Thirdly, you will have documentation of the Scripture verses He leads you to. Furthermore, you preserve the exact words from God's mouth, so your enemy can't twist them around, and use them against you later. These are just a few of the benefits of journaling your interaction with God.

The Holy Spirit of God reveals His thoughts to me, and I don't want to miss one of them. Amos 4:13 says, "He who forms the mountains, creates the wind, and *reveals His thoughts to man*, He who turns dawn to darkness, and treads the high places of the earth—the Lord God Almighty is His name" (emphasis mine). When Almighty God speaks, everyone should stand up and listen! If the Creator of the universe, the Most High God, articulates His thoughts to His creation, we ought to preserve them in written form, just as His chosen followers and disciples did in Bible times.

Every time I meet with God, I write down our conversation. He already knows my thoughts and questions, but I usually write them down anyway in a notebook or on the computer. Then I wait to hear Him speak. While I'm waiting to hear His voice, I journal every thought popping into my head, no matter how unusual or unimportant it seems. *Why?* Recording all my thoughts offers me the best chance of discerning the still, small voice of God from the other voices in my head.

In journaling my conversations with God, at times I find myself frantically scribbling all the thoughts pouring into my brain. Before I know it, my pen takes over and just keeps writing everything I hear. As I go back and read what I have written, I can see where my own thoughts end and God's begin. While my thoughts lack confidence and certainty, His thoughts are authoritative and convicting. My expressions are timid and self-condemning, but God's voice exudes strength and encouragement. My ways are naïve and simple, while His ways are wise and wonderful. Many times God speaks words to me I long to hear, and I wonder, *Are these my own self-soothing thoughts, or does God really speak to me this way?* But every time I re-read in my notes what God said, the reassuring peace and confirmation of knowing I'm enjoying sweet fellowship with my wonderful Savior rushes over me. I know these words are not my own cognitive concoctions. Being able to distinguish your own thoughts from the thoughts of the Holy Spirit is crucial.

Since the Holy Spirit reminds us of God's Word, you will know the Spirit speaks to you when you recognize a concept or verse from the Bible infused with the words you have written in your journal. You will recognize God's voice in your notes as He speaks to you in a loving, encouraging, affirming manner. His voice will be apparent when you feel conviction of a sin and when He speaks the truth in love. Read God's encouragement in this example from my own journal:

Journal Entry on 04/15/2004

My child, I have called you My own. You belong to Me. Do you cherish Me the same way I cherish you? You are everything to Me. I have engraved you on the palms of My hands. Your name is burned into My mind. You are always on My heart. I will never forget you. Try writing My name on your palms and do not forget Me.

Remember what I say to you. Write it down. Draw on it when times are tough. Refer back to it when it becomes difficult for you to hear Me. It will help you recall what I have said to you. I have written so many things on your heart. I have written so many things in My Word. You have My written Word to help you find your way; you have My Holy Spirit to remind you of what I have said. The words spoken by My Spirit within you will lead you back to My written Word. Write down the words I put in your mind and on your heart. Examine them again as needed.

Life gets crazy. A time may come when you do not hear Me. Then you will refer back to your journal and relive the words I have spoken to you. Cling tightly to the spoken and written words I have given you. You will cherish the time we spent together in the past and allow My voice to be heard in your mind and heart once more.

You are My beloved child. I have so much wisdom to send your way. Be diligent in recording the knowledge I impart. Do not take it lightly. It may save you some day. Record everything you hear, big or small. Sometimes the biggest blessings are wrapped in the smallest packages. Record every thought that presents itself in your head. When the words begin to flow more rapidly, you will recognize

My hand in it. When you look at it again, you will be able to discern your own thoughts from My thoughts in your journal writings.

Anything worth anything is worth writing down. Write down anything and everything I say to you.

As God mentioned in the above entry, my journal becomes really useful when I experience times of spiritual drought—when I feel disconnect from God, when He doesn't speak to me, or when I can't hear Him. Then I return to the pages where I wrote down His whispers and re-read previous conversations I had with Him. It brings me comfort and encouragement and sends me in a positive direction each time I read them. I'm able to reconnect with God and remember what it sounds like to hear from Him. It helps me remember His character and how He feels toward me. It's a way to reconnect my spirit with the Spirit of God inside me.

Honestly, there are times in my life when I just don't make time to meet with God. If too much time goes by, I empathize with the prodigal son. Guilt takes over, and I worry God will be mad at me and not speak to me again. I soon realize Satan wants me to feel guilty and believe this lie. Truly, every time I return to God after not speaking with Him for weeks at a time, we pick up right where we left off. God does not punish me for my lack of commitment. He cherishes the time I give Him and speaks to me like an old friend and a beloved child. Re-reading what I have written in my journal reminds me of God's faithfulness and unconditional love.

Pausing to listen for His voice is vital. How can I hear Him speak if I don't leave room in the conversation for Him? Write down your comments or questions to God, and then lift your pen off the paper for a few moments to wait for His response. You may write a paragraph or two, but leave Him space on the page to reply. Do not feel the need to fill the air with your own voice and thoughts all the time. Learn to become comfortable with the silence. Ecclesiastes states, "There is a time for everything, and a season for every activity under heaven: …a time to be silent and a time to speak" (Ecclesiastes 3:1, 7).

Clear your mind of all the clutter and obstructions. As I said earlier, if random thoughts enter your mind—like your grocery shopping list or your "to do" list for the day—quickly jot them down so you won't forget them, and then return your focus to God. Concentrate on the topic of your discussion. Reiterate your questions or comments to Him. Then write down the next thoughts that enter your mind—all of them, no matter how common or strange they may seem. Sometimes you will find abundant meaning in the simplest expressions.

Documenting what you hear God say to you will be monumental in your quest for intimacy with Him. With all the distractions we have pulling us away from God, taking time to read through your journal of His messages to you will put you back on track in focusing your attention in His direction. The ability to read and reread His loving, encouraging words, specifically given to you, will build your confidence in your relationship with Him, just like reading His message of love for you in the Bible does.

Had the scribes not put their time and attention into writing down the inspired words of God, we would not have the Bible today. If you do not write down what He says to you, those words may get lost in your head, and you may not be able to recall them exactly as

He gave them to you. Satan would love to twist and mix up the words God has given you to make you believe his version instead. Just as you use the sword of the Spirit, the Word of God, to battle your enemy, you may also use the truth in God's words you have written down in your journal to fight the one who opposes you. What God says to you will be reinforced by Scripture.

When you learn to distinguish God's voice, or thoughts, as you are journaling your conversation with Him, write His voice in cursive or italics, and print your thoughts to distinguish the two voices on paper. When possible, date each conversation. Title your journal entry with a fitting name to identify the topic, so it's easier to spot when you want to return to it later.

If you don't care for the practice of journaling or if you often communicate with God while you are driving, you may want to utilize a hand-held digital recording device or a smartphone app to capture your words, as well as the words He speaks to you. Most people do not hear an audible voice of God. The most common way He speaks to us is by interjecting His thoughts into our minds. Because of this, you'll have to repeat all the thoughts you hear from

Him into the recorder. Later, you may personally transcribe the recording into a notebook or use an internet service to transcribe your conversations with God for safekeeping.

Maybe you love to blog. When your conversations with God are not too personal, consider posting them in some form. You can tweak them to be more generic and allow others to enjoy a word from the Lord. If you don't yet have a blog, you may set one up free on Wordpress.org or Wordpress.com. I maintain a blog on my website, **www.sindynagel.com**. The posts filed under the category titled "From God's Heart to Yours" come from messages I hear from God and relay to you. Here's a sample:

Life in the Son

Lord, I have been in a slump because of the dreary weather. Would You shine some light into my life? Does the sun, or the lack of it, really make that big of a difference in my life?

My child, if only you knew. Life in the Son makes a monumental difference. The sun I have placed in the sky may lift your spirits while it shines, but it does not provide constant light, as you know. Truly, My Son will shine His light into your darkness at all hours of the day and night. You never need to endure the storms of life alone. I am with you always. I will shine My light of life into every dark corner. I will light the way for you. I will lead you in the path of life.

My sweet daughter, life in the Son does make a big difference. Even on the darkest of days, you may have joy in your heart because you belong to Me. I am the true light that gives life. As you walk in the rain, My light will lead you on your way. Follow Me and you will never walk in darkness, because I am the light of life. (See John 8:12.) I have made My light shine in your heart to give you the light of the knowledge of the glory of God in the face of Christ. (See 2 Corinthians 4:6.)

My precious one, life in the Son does make a big difference. You may be downcast for a little while, but consider what I have done for you. I am light. I have given you My light. In Me there is no darkness. (See 1 John 1:5.) Never again will you remain in darkness, because you believe in Me, the light of the world.

Are you downcast? Look to Me for your happiness. Are your spirits low? I will lift you up on eagle's wings. Are you depressed? I will remove your sackcloth and clothe you with joy. Are you stuck in a pit? I will pull you out and place you on solid ground. Are you caught in the middle of a storm? I will weather it with you and bring you to a place of rest. I am with you.

Seek Me, My child, and I will give you joy in your spirit and peace in your heart. My light will illuminate the darkest of days. Even as we speak, the skies are getting brighter. I have come into the world as a light, so that no one who believes in Me shall stay in darkness (John 12:46). Life in the Son does make a big difference. Choose the light of life.

The gift of the Holy Spirit and the ability to hear God's voice are like having your own Bible, personalized just for you. At all times and in all places, you have access to God's will and word through His Spirit inside you. The Holy Spirit takes the words of God and Jesus and makes them known to you. Listen to the inspired word of God inside you, and write it down. You'll be thankful you have the opportunity to refer back to God's personal words for you at a later date. Each word He utters has value and may connect to other things He reveals to you later. The thoughts God gives you one day may make sense down the road a month or two later. You may ask God a question or pray a prayer He doesn't answer for several days, weeks, months, even years. Recording your conversations will allow you to track and relate one to another, as God uncovers His will, plan, and purpose for your life.

Rejoice whether you hear one word, four sentences, or two paragraphs from the mouth of the Lord. Each and every word God speaks to you is precious and valuable. Sometimes the most priceless things God says are one-word expressions. Don't compare how He speaks to you with how He speaks to your friend. He communicates with you exactly the way you can hear Him with exactly the word(s) you need to hear—no more, no less. Write down every word God says to you while you practice the art of listening to His voice.

STEP 4 - SELF-REFLECTION:

1. List three benefits to recording your conversations with God.

2. Would you prefer to document your time with God by writing by hand in a notebook or by typing your conversations on the computer?

3. How would recording your conversations help you distinguish God's thoughts from your own and Satan's thoughts?

4. How will you differentiate your thoughts from God's in your journal? For example, print vs. *italics*? Black ink vs. colored ink? Plain vs. highlighted?

STEP 4 – WRITE IT DOWN

5. Do you relate to feeling like a prodigal child when you do not regularly spend time with God? Does that cause disconnect in your relationship with Him?

6. How would re-reading your conversations with God help you re-connect with Him?

7. If you don't like the idea of journaling, describe another way you could capture the words of God for future reference.

7-DAY CHALLENGE:

Hold onto your conversations with God this week by writing down what you hear. Print your thoughts and questions to God, then lift your pen off the page. Sit quietly and wait for His response to you. Record the very next thought(s) you have or word(s) you hear in your head. Ask God for more clarification or confirmation of what you just heard. Continue to record all the words or thoughts the Holy Spirit communicates to you. If you are unsure it is God speaking to you, read over your writing and highlight words, phrases, or ideas that may have been from God. Use the concordance in your Bible to lookup verses that relate to the topic of your conversation. When a verse stands out to you, find that verse and read over the related

Scripture passage. The Holy Spirit will make things known to you through God's Word. Does this verse solidify or confirm what God spoke to you in your thoughts? The next chapter provides more instruction on discerning God's voice.

STEP 5

PRACTICE DAILY

Some words in the English language can be used as both verbs and nouns; for example, the word "practice." The verb form of "practice" is synonymous with the following terms: do, live out, try, follow, attempt, perform, rehearse, prepare, and exercise. The noun form of "practice" is synonymous with: ritual, system, habit, and routine.[1] You can be successful at hearing God's voice when you practice a practice: perform a ritual, attempt to live out a system, rehearse a routine, or exercise a habit.

When pondering the word "practice," what comes to my mind immediately is a sports team. I spent many evenings and Saturdays chauffeuring my children to their sports practices and games. In order for a team to be successful, the members need to practice, that is, perform and repeat their skills both individually and together. If you want to be good at something, anything, you must practice, or rehearse, whatever skill you desire to develop. Olympians make "practicing" their career; they work daily at becoming the best they can be. Anyone who plays an instrument or creates an art form also knows the value of practicing. Becoming the best you can at hearing God's voice requires that you practice, practice, practice. Hearing from God is an amazing experience. Don't give up! Keep trying! Of course, no one will ever be *perfect*, but we can work at *perfect*ing our skill of listening to God. Practicing daily does make progress. Be the best you can be and practice daily listening to God.

When I first attempted to listen to God, I did not have a clue where to begin or what exactly I needed to do. I didn't know how to go about it, other than what my mentor had suggested: sitting quietly and writing down what I heard. The first time I succeeded at hearing God's voice, He dangled the carrot in front of me. He enticed me by allowing me to hear His voice so I would continue to be hungry for more of Him. The next several times I attempted to hear His voice

STEP 5 – PRACTICE DAILY

did not result in success, however. Did God not speak to me again right away, or did I need more practice to hear Him?

Listening to God is an art that may not come naturally, a skill that needs to be developed. I had to practice sitting quietly and journaling my thoughts until I achieved the knack of hearing God speak. When I first started listening for His voice, many times I heard nothing. Here's the key to my success: **I didn't give up.** I continued to practice the ritual, or routine, of getting up early every morning to sit quietly before the Lord and attempt to listen to Him speak to me. Time after time, I heard nothing, but I didn't quit. I knew I had heard God speak to me once, and I yearned for more. I knew if I kept trying, I would hear Him again. My persistence and perseverance eventually paid off.

Sitting in silence every morning proved to be a challenge. First of all, I knew I might not hear from God that day. Getting up extra early caused me to miss out on my beauty sleep. That could be dangerous for my family, right? The knowledge that it might be a waste of good slumber time fed the overwhelming desire to stay in bed when the alarm went off. Secondly, I felt like I wasted valuable time that could be used for accomplishing something else I needed to do that day. Thirdly, I found it hard to focus because distracting thoughts cluttered my mind. My brain replayed conversations I'd had the day before. I made a mental list of all the things I needed to do. I pondered the meal I would prepare that night. I did anything I could do to fill the void, the silence in my head. I asked God for the things I needed. I filled the quietness with my own voice instead of waiting patiently for Him to take His turn. But how can we expect to hear His voice if we do not practice leaving room in the conversation for Him?

The key to communicating well is to practice the art of listening well. God gave us two ears and one mouth, so we would listen twice as much as we speak. In our conversations with Him, we need to be good listeners. If we really desire to hear Him speak and share His wisdom with us, it's imperative we listen more than we talk. Are you a good listener?

Being an active listener enables us to hear God speak. Be active by writing down what you hear, all the thoughts going through your head. Repeat to God what He says to you. Ask God to confirm that what you hear is from Him. Use the Bible to verify and enhance what you hear God say. Look up verses related to the words He speaks to you, and write down what the Spirit reveals to you through the Scripture. Ask God for more information. Praise Him enthusiastically with your full attention when you meet.

Initially, when I did more talking than listening, I occasionally heard a word or a short phrase I thought might be from God. I wrote down His words, but I didn't expect that God would communicate at length with me. Still, I knew I had to practice extra periods of time where I just sat still and listened. When I intentionally spent more time listening than speaking, I heard sentences, and then paragraphs, and then pages. Practicing good listening skills is absolutely vital in hearing God speak.

Of course, some days I did not listen at all. I had so much to say to God that only my own voice filled the time. Yet I know had I listened, God would have spoken to me. On the days I ran out of time to hear from God, my own monopolization of the conversation disappointed me fiercely. The next day I would deliberately exercise more self-control to leave gaps in the dialogue, waiting patiently to hear God speak. Quiet time with Him means just that—being quiet as you meet with Him. Rehearsing silence as you spend time with the Lord affords Him the opportunity to reveal what's on His mind. What's on God's mind is more meaningful and spectacular than many things I might have to say.

Hearing God's voice could be compared to winning a championship trophy—receiving a reward or a prize for obedience. It changed my life completely. All the practice sessions paid off. God honored my time and diligence with the ability to hear Him speak. Jesus, the One who had pursued me all these years, now became the object of my pursuit. I delighted myself in the Lord, and He gave me the desires of my heart (see Psalm 37:4). I searched for God as for hidden treasure, and He remunerated me with the gift of intimacy with Jesus Christ, my Savior and Redeemer.

Another necessary element to clearly hearing God's voice is practicing discernment. The first time I heard God's voice in my thoughts, it took me by surprise. I had never considered that one of the other voices *or thoughts* in my head might be God's. Neither did I realize that some of the other voices *or thoughts* in my head belonged to my enemy, Satan. Correctly discerning God's voice from Satan's voice is crucial in the practice of listening to God. To discern God's voice from Satan's voice requires us to learn more about the character of God and the character of Satan. Make sure all your thoughts are obedient to Christ. Learn all that you can about the object of your affection. Immerse yourself in the Bible; study the One you follow. Listen to His voice in Scripture—what His words sound like—so you will be equipped to identify His voice when He speaks to you in your thoughts.

On the next page is a list of some of my favorite characteristics of God and where they are found in the Bible. But don't take my word for it. Dig into God's Word yourself, and let Him show you His character. Come up with a list of your favorite characteristics of God.

Know God's Character

Compassionate, gracious, slow to anger, abounding in love and faithfulness	Exodus 34:6
Forgives wickedness, rebellion, and sin	Exodus 34:7
Immanuel – God with us	Matthew 1:23
Everlasting God, Creator, does not grow tired or weary	Isaiah 40:28
The way, the truth, the life	John 14:6
Good Shepherd	John 10:14
Father, Son, and Holy Spirit	Galatians 4:6
Alpha and Omega, First and Last, Beginning and End	Revelation 22:13
Light of the world	John 8:12
Rock, Fortress, Deliverer, Shield, Stronghold, Refuge, Savior	2 Samuel 22:2-3
Wonderful Counselor, Mighty God, Everlasting Father, Prince of Peace	Isaiah 9:6
God is Love; He lives in us	1 John 4:16, Galatians 4:6
Counselor, Spirit of truth	John 14:16-17
Healer, Restorer, Guide	Psalm 147:3, Psalm 23:3
Never leaves us or forgets us	Joshua 1:5

God's messages to you will be filled with His Word from the Bible. Verses will come alive to you every time you read it, because the voice of God within you directs you back to Scripture and offers newfound clarity for you and your life. Hebrews 4:12 says, "For the Word of God is living and active. Sharper than any double-edged sword, it penetrates even to dividing soul and spirit, joints and marrow; it judges the thoughts and attitudes of the heart." The primary way God still speaks to His children is through His living, active Word.

God's words are usually very loving and gentle, while at the same time exuding strength and firmness. They are convicting, not condemning. They are words of endearment and encouragement. They produce immeasurable peace within me. God's words bring me comfort and emotional healing. They are always true and always align with His Word and His character in the Bible. Sometimes God's words motivate me and stir me into action to carry out His will. Whenever I've acted on the promptings of the Holy Spirit of God, I've experienced an immeasurable, lasting joy.

Don't be afraid to ask God for more clarification. Ask Him to confirm that what you just heard came from Him. He may say it to you again and verify it for you. Or you may need to seek confirmation in the Bible or from a trusted friend. God may confirm His whispers through a sermon your pastor preaches, the words of a song on Christian radio, or in a Christian book you are reading. Be sure to check it out further. As many times as you ask for more confirmation, our patient God authenticates what He speaks to you.

Also, we must know more about the ways of Satan in order to distinguish his voice from God's in our thoughts. To get a better picture of Satan's character, let's look at some verses in Scripture that refer to his nature and his actions. See the table below.

Know the Character and Ways of Satan

He is a roaring lion, looking for someone to devour	1 Peter 5:8-9
Murderer, liar, father of lies	John 8:44
The devil tempts us	Matthew 4:1
He speaks to us and uses Scripture to deceive us	Matthew 4:5-7
Satan masquerades as an angel of light and his servants masquerade as servants of righteousness	2 Corinthians 11:14-15
Messengers of Satan are sent as thorns in the flesh to torment us	2 Corinthians 12:7
He sows evil in the world	Matthew 13:36-39
He takes away the word that was sown in us	Mark 4:15
He prompts our spirits to sin and commit evil	John 13:2
Anger not dealt with gives the devil a foothold	Ephesians 4:26-27
He traps us and holds us captive to do his will	2 Timothy 2:24-26
He is the deceiver, the antichrist	2 John 7
He possesses people with demons and evil spirits	Luke 4:33
Satan entered Judas Iscariot to betray Jesus	Luke 22:3
He asks to sift us like wheat	Luke 22:31-32
Satan fell like lightning from heaven	Luke 10:18
He holds us in slavery by our fear of death	Hebrews 2:15
He has been sinning from the beginning	1 John 3:8
Satan and his angels lost their place in heaven	Revelation 12:8
The great dragon, ancient serpent called the devil or	Revelation 12:9

STEP 5 – PRACTICE DAILY

Satan, who leads the world astray	
The accuser	Revelation 12:10
Satan is filled with fury	Revelation 12:12
He pursues women	Revelation 12:13
The devil wages war against us	Revelation 12:17
The devil schemes against us	Ephesians 6:11
He is the ruler, authority, power of this dark world, spiritual force of evil in the heavenly realms	Ephesians 6:12
The evil one attacks us with flaming arrows	Ephesians 6:16

Consider the Bible verses cited in the table above. Some are written out below to further describe our spiritual opponent and how he operates. Notice some of the verses also instruct us how to battle against the enemy. The words in *italics* are my emphasis of the devil's ways.

> Be self-controlled and alert. Your enemy the devil *prowls around* like a roaring lion, looking for someone to *devour*. Resist him, standing firm in the faith, because you know that your brothers throughout the world are undergoing the same kind of sufferings. (1 Peter 5:8-9)

> He was a *murderer* from the beginning, not holding to the truth, for there is no truth in Him. When he lies, he speaks his native language, for he is *a liar* and the father of lies. (John 8:44)

> Then the devil took Him to the holy city and had Him stand on the highest point of the temple. "If You are the Son of God," he said, "*throw Yourself down*. For it is written: 'He will command His angels concerning You, and they will lift You up in their hands, so that

You will not strike Your foot against a stone.'" Jesus answered him, "It is also written: 'Do not put the Lord your God to the test.'" (Matthew 4:5-7)

And no wonder, for Satan himself *masquerades as an angel of light*. It is not surprising, then, if *his servants masquerade as servants of righteousness*. Their end will be what their actions deserve. (2 Corinthians 11:14-15)

Jesus told them another parable: "The kingdom of heaven is like a man who sowed good seed in His field. But while everyone was sleeping, His *enemy came and sowed weeds* among the wheat, and went away." (Matthew 13:24-25)

Then He left the crowd and went into the house. His disciples came to Him and said, "Explain to us the parable of the weeds in the field." He answered, "The one who sowed the good seed is the Son of Man. The field is the world, and the good seed stands for the sons of the kingdom. The *weeds are the sons of the evil one*, and the *enemy who sows* them is the devil." (Matthew 13:36-39)

The evening meal was being served and the devil had already *prompted* Judas Iscariot, son of Simon, to betray Jesus. (John 13:2)

In your anger do not sin: Do not let the sun go down while you are still angry, and do not give the devil a *foothold.* (Ephesians 4:26-27)

Submit yourselves, then, to God. Resist the devil, and he will flee from you. Come near to God and He will come near to you. (James 4:7-8)

And the Lord's servant must not quarrel; instead, he must be kind to everyone, able to teach, not resentful. Those who oppose him he must gently instruct, in the hope that God will grant them repentance leading them to a knowledge of the truth, and that they will come to their senses and escape the *trap of the devil*, who has *taken them captive* to do His will. (2 Timothy 2:24-26)

Since the children have flesh and blood, He too shared in their humanity so that by His death He might destroy him who *holds the power of death*—that is, the devil—and free those who all their lives were *held in slavery* by their fear of death. For surely it is not angels He helps, but Abraham's descendants. For this reason He had to be made like His brothers in every way, in order that He might become a merciful and faithful high priest in service to God, and that He might make atonement for the sins of the people. Because He Himself suffered when He *was tempted*, He is able to help those who are being tempted. (Hebrews 2:14-18)

Many *deceivers*, who do *not acknowledge Jesus Christ* as coming in the flesh, have gone out into the world. Any such person is the deceiver and *the antichrist*. Watch out that you do not lose what you have worked for, but that you may be rewarded fully. (2 John 7-8)

Jesus said, "Simon, Simon, Satan has asked to *sift you* as wheat. But I have prayed for you, Simon, that your faith may not fail. And when you have turned back, strengthen your brothers." (Luke 22:31-32)

The *great dragon* was hurled down—that the *ancient serpent* called the devil or Satan, who *leads the whole world astray*. He was hurled to the earth, and his angels with Him. Then I heard a loud voice in heaven say:

"Now have come the salvation and the power and the kingdom of our God, and the authority of His Christ. For the *accuser* of our brothers, who *accuses them* before our God day and night, has been hurled down. They overcame him by the blood of the Lamb and by the word of their testimony; they did not love their lives so much as to shrink from death. Therefore rejoice, you heavens and you who dwell in them! But woe to the earth and the sea, because the devil has gone down to you! He is *filled with fury*, because he knows that his time is short."

When the dragon saw that he had been hurled to earth, he *pursued the woman* who had given birth to the male child. The woman was given the two wings of a great eagle, so that she might fly to the place prepared for her in the desert, where she would be taken care of for a time, times and half a time, out of the serpent's reach. Then from His mouth the serpent spewed water like a river, to *overtake the woman* and sweep her away with the torrent. But the earth helped the woman by opening its mouth and swallowing the river that the dragon had spewed out of his mouth. Then the dragon was *enraged at the woman* and went off to *make war against the rest of her offspring*—those who obey God's commandments and hold to the testimony of Jesus. (Revelation 12:9-17)

> Finally, be strong in the Lord and in His mighty power. Put on the full armor of God so that you can take your stand against the *devil's schemes*. For our struggle is not against flesh and blood, but against the *rulers,* against the *authorities*, against the *powers of this dark world* and against the *spiritual forces of evil* in the heavenly realms. Therefore put on the full armor of God, so that when the day of evil comes, you may be able to stand your ground, and after you have done everything, to stand. Stand firm then, with the belt of truth buckled around your waist, with the breastplate of righteousness in place, and with your feet fitted with the readiness that comes from the gospel of peace. In addition to all this, take up the shield of faith, with which you can extinguish all the *flaming arrows of the evil one*. Take the helmet of salvation and the sword of the Spirit, which is the word of God. And pray in the Spirit on all occasions with all kinds of prayers and requests. With this in mind, be alert and always keep on praying for all the saints. (Ephesians 6:10-18)

It's not my intent to frighten you about your spiritual enemy. I simply want to make you aware of and alert to the devil's ways. Also, it is not my intent to give the devil more power than God gives him. Simply know this: When you become more intentional about pursuing a deeper relationship with Jesus Christ, you will most assuredly place a bigger target on your back for the devil to take his aim. When you maximize your offense, bringing your A game in relating to God, you must increase your awareness and your defense against your spiritual opponent, too. Satan's investment in lukewarm

Christians is minimal in comparison to his zealous endeavors to derail those who actively seek perpetual intimacy with God.

Don't let this keep you from chasing passionately after God. Jesus Christ already won the victory in the battle over your heart. Simply claim your victory over Satan in the name of Jesus Christ, your Savior, by His authority and His blood. In John 14:14, Jesus says, "You may ask Me for anything in My name and I will do it." Fight your spiritual opponent by calling on the name of Jesus Christ, claiming aloud your defeat over Satan with Christ's power and authority. Declare the truth of Scripture to defeat Satan and to encourage yourself, standing firm in the faith.

Dress yourself in the armor of God, as described in Ephesians 6:10-18, by praying this Scripture as you verbalize putting on each piece of protective armor. Be alert and rebuke the devil whenever he strikes. As stated in James 4:7, "Resist the devil, and he will flee from you." Arm yourself with the Word of God by memorizing verses that effectively speak against Satan's attack on your weak spots, and be ready to use these verses against Him. The devil does *not* know your thoughts, so speak out loud to Satan as you battle him with Scripture. Pray on all occasions for God's protection. Remember, the same power that raised Jesus Christ from the dead is the power that lives in you. In the name of Jesus, you have authority over the devil. Luke 10:17-20 says,

> The seventy-two returned with joy and said, "Lord, even the demons submit to us in Your name." He replied, "I saw Satan fall like lightning from heaven. I have given you authority to trample on snakes and scorpions and to overcome all the power of the enemy; nothing will harm you. However, do not rejoice that the spirits submit to you, but rejoice that your names are written in heaven."

Now that we have studied the character of God and the character of Satan, let's examine the difference between God's voice and Satan's voice. First, you should know our omniscient God knows all of our thoughts, but Satan knows none of them. He acts based only on his perception and observations of our actions and responses to particular situations. That's why it's so important to declare the truth of Scripture *out loud*. Since Satan can't read your mind, it's vital to verbalize *aloud* your intentions to resist the devil and walk in victory. Secondly, but no less importantly, remember God lives inside us and Satan lives outside of us. The moment we accept Christ as our Savior, God sends His Spirit to live inside of us.

Third, God and Satan may both speak to us in our thoughts, but that's where the similarity stops. A definite difference between the two voices exists. The tables on this page and the next page show the contrast when discerning God's voice from Satan's.

Discern What You Hear

God's Voice	Satan's Voice
Loving	Unloving
Sincere	Conniving
Encouraging	Disapproving
Peaceful	Disturbing
Comforting	Disrupting
Healing	Wounding
Truthful	Deceitful, Lying
Clear, Precise	Confusing
Motivating	Provoking
Aligns with Scripture	Uses Scripture to Deceive
Uplifting	Condescending
Commending	Accusing
Positive	Negative
Forthright	Manipulative
Purifying	Clouding
Refining	Distorting
Gentle	Harsh
Strong, Firm	Indecisive
Redeeming	Shaming
Convicting	Condemning

STEP 5 – PRACTICE DAILY

Discern Who You Hear

God	Satan
Stills you	Rushes you
Reassures you	Frightens you
Leads you	Pushes you
Enlightens you	Confuses you
Forgives you	Condemns you
Calms you	Stresses you
Encourages you	Discourages you
Comforts you	Worries you
Inspires you	Deters you
Frees you	Traps you
Uplifts you	Degrades you
Adores you	Mocks you
Loves you	Hates you
Redeems you	Shames you

Learn to recognize God's voice vs. Satan's. Your own thoughts are mixed in, too. For the most part, when God speaks, you'll feel His peace in your soul. The exception is when the Spirit stirs you to conviction of a sin or points out something you need to change. Again, this will be a spirit of conviction, not condemnation, and not guilt-producing after you repent. The initial conviction by the Spirit may cause feelings of guilt to rise up in you. However, when you confess your sin, ask for forgiveness, and fully accept God's grace and forgiveness, you will ultimately feel peace and freedom. Any further thoughts or feelings of guilt and shame for this confessed sin are projected from Satan, not God. When the Holy Spirit inside you makes you aware of a sin in your life you need to confess, a behavior you need to change, an action you need to take, or something else that matters to God, be quick to respond with a grateful heart and obedience to His prompting.

God's voice speaks kindness and blessing mixed with conviction about how I could be doing better. It's *not* condemning me, saying, "You are a bad person." I bought in to those lies for too long. For nearly thirty-five years, Satan held me captive by the lie that I was not wanted and not loved. God had to free me from bondage, like He freed the Israelites from slavery, before I could worship Him wholeheartedly. Is something holding you back from worshiping God with total freedom? What holds you captive today?

Break free from it with the power of the Holy Spirit, in the name of Jesus Christ. Allow Jesus, the Savior, to deliver you from the hands of your opponent. Strive to know more about God and Satan. When you are aware of the difference in their characteristics, actions, tones, and methods, you will better recognize where your thoughts originate. Discern God's voice and hold on to the truth. Discern Satan's voice and refuse to believe the lies. Whatever remains are your own thoughts. Make sure they are pleasing to God. Practice discernment when listening to God.

Hearing God's voice is absolutely life-changing. Jesus as your best friend and advocate is all you need. Nothing else matters more. When a sports team wins the championship trophy, they celebrate all the fruits of their labor. They realize the reward of the months and years of practice and hard work. Good things come to those who are diligent. Be diligent at listening to God. Make it your lifetime goal, your priority, and your purpose to recognize when God speaks to you. Your awareness of His voice will increase when your ears are tuned toward Him more regularly. You will recognize His expressions in your thoughts more frequently. The content of your two-way conversations will grow deeper as you practice vulnerable transparency, confiding in the One who created you for His pleasure and will. Then listen attentively to His response.

Put in the time and effort, and God will reward you with the ability to hear His voice. Then celebrate the fruit of your labor. The fruit of God's Spirit within you is love, both given and received. Unending joy and inevitable peace are products of living in step with the Spirit. Tuning into the voice of God within you takes practice, and the practice of listening to God's voice drives you to realize the longings of your soul. The ultimate goal and reward are one and the same—hearing God's voice. The practice of listening to God's voice will return abundant rewards for your enjoyment. We'll briefly explore seven rewards of hearing from God in the next chapter.

STEP 5 - SELF-REFLECTION:

1. Have you ever participated in a sport, hobby, or activity that required practice to become more proficient? If so, how many hours did you practice to increase your skill?

2. How much time are you willing to spend practicing to develop your skill of hearing God's voice?

3. Thinking about God's character, how would you expect His voice in your thoughts to sound?

4. Reviewing Satan's character, how would you expect his voice in your thoughts to sound?

5. How do you battle the thoughts from Satan in your mind?

6. How do you confirm the thoughts from God?

7. How do you plan to strengthen and deepen your relationship with Jesus?

7-DAY CHALLENGE:

As you practice listening to God this week, be aware that your enemy, the devil, may focus more of his attention on you, trying to derail your efforts for intimacy with God. He will also introduce or reiterate lies he wants you to believe. Be more intentional about taking all your thoughts captive and discerning God's voice from Satan's. Using what you know about the character and ways of Satan, expose and reveal ideas and promptings from him. Find Scripture verses that you can repeat aloud to battle the enemy. Stand firm in the power and victory of Jesus Christ and profess it out loud. The One living in you is greater than the one living in the world. Pray the protection of God's armor over yourself and your loved ones (See Ephesians 6:10-18). Resist the devil, and he will flee from you. (James 4:7)

Treasure the thoughts you hear from God. Praise Him for the gift of close relationship with the living God dwelling in you. Celebrate and enjoy the rewards of discerning God's voice in your thoughts as they are revealed in the next chapter.

STEP 6

ENJOY THE REWARDS

Hearing God's voice for the first time resembles discovering a buried treasure. God's amazing treasure chest holds at least seven priceless jewels. Below, we'll uncover and explore these seven rewards. Also, watch for my forthcoming book, *7 Rewards of Hearing God's Voice*.

7 Rewards of Hearing God's Voice

- Healing
- Forgiveness
- Encouragement
- Instruction
- Conviction
- Wisdom
- Peace

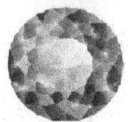

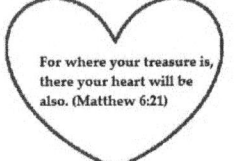

For where your treasure is, there your heart will be also. (Matthew 6:21)

Reward #1 - Absorb the Healing

My first depression plagued me most severely. I didn't know the symptoms, so it took me nearly five months to realize, and then admit, depression had seized me. By that time, I had tumbled to rock bottom. The word *shattered* best describes the way depression feels to me. Try to imagine a car that has been in an accident. What do you see? I see a windshield that has been shattered into hundreds of pieces and is held together only by the window frame. Similarly, in depression I felt shattered into a thousand pieces on the inside, held together only by my skin. No one knew depression tormented me. I appeared completely normal from the outside, but I felt weak, fragile, and broken on the inside. Looking back, I now know God allowed me to hit rock bottom so I had nowhere else to turn but to Him.

Once I admitted my unhealthy emotional state, I sought medical help and counseling. I started taking antidepressant medication and met with a psychologist once each week for over a year. Through Christian counseling, God showed me what kept me from the life He intended for me. I had to confront my past. I had to be delivered from the bondage of my belief in Satan's lies before I could effectively relate to God and worship Him with all my heart. I did the work of digging into my childhood to figure out what caused me to be stuck in this life.

We all have emotional wounds. Some of them are given to us by people we love and people who love us. My most major emotional wound came from believing lies in the words my mom used about me. I'm sure she didn't intend to wound me, but Satan used the things she said to deceive me into believing his lies. As a young girl, I remember my mom telling other people of me, "She was an accident." I heard my mom say I was an accident many, many times. Those words stabbed deep into my heart. Those words gave me my identity:

I am an accident. I am not wanted. I am not loved.

Notice how Satan used those words, "You are an accident," and twisted them to accuse me of his lies: "You are not wanted; you are not loved." Remember John 8:44? Jesus exposed the devil's ways: "When he lies, he speaks his native language, for he is a liar and the father of lies." The enemy wanted me to believe lies that would keep me in bondage so I could not become all God wanted me to be, and I fell for it like a boulder plummeting down a mountainside.

Knowing I was unwanted caused me to become a people-pleaser. My entire life was driven by my desire to be needed and loved. My constant striving to satisfy and delight everyone required me to give large chunks of myself away. The more I gave, the more empty, unloved, and unappreciated I felt. My zest for life slowly drained out of me, leaving me unfulfilled and unhappy. I had a decent life, but if it equaled the life God had planned for me, I wasn't sure I wanted to live. I had everything I needed and wanted, yet I lacked something. What I had was not enough to carry me through emotionally.

By believing the father of lies, I had let the deceit of Satan rule in my heart. God allowed me to experience depression so I would seek Him for help, answers, and healing. God wanted me to confront the emotional wounds from my past so He could wrap me in His blanket of light. God used my counseling as the venue where He performed the emotional healing I needed.

My counselor and I would spend time in prayer, bringing my wounds before Christ and asking Him to replace the lies I believed with the truth. Jesus showed me His presence in my childhood memories. He Himself told me of His great love for me and revealed the truth about me and the circumstances of my birth. He crushed the lies of the enemy. God planned me from the beginning; I was no accident. He wanted me and loved me.

This experience compelled me to trust Jesus even more. He is the way, the truth, and the life. The voice of Jesus in my memories transformed my life. When you are set straight by the God of the universe, it's a permanent healing. It's a healing you can't get from counseling alone or from anything anyone else says to you. When God Himself meets you in your memories, shows you His presence in your life, speaks about how much He loves you, and couples it with strong, truthful feelings in your heart, it changes everything.

My beliefs about my own identity began to change. It no longer mattered that my mom didn't want me, because the God of the universe planned me before He created the world. He wants me and loves me. I am His child, created in His image. I am a high priority to Him. My existence is important to Him. He wants to spend forever showing me how much He loves me. I know He feels the same about you.

God *does* speak to *you* in your thoughts. He can use your memories to bring you healing and to show you His presence throughout your whole life. Come to Him, and quiet yourself enough to listen to what He has to say. He will enlighten you with His truth, replacing the darkness of the lies you believe. In John 8:36, Jesus says, "So if the Son sets you free, you will be free indeed." I live a new life of freedom—a better life—because Christ set me free from my emotional prison, the bondage of the lies I held onto. That's what Jesus came here to do—to "set the captives free." (See Isaiah 61:1-3.) He is the truth.

Jesus Christ already won the battle over Satan, sin, and death with His obedience even unto death on the cross. God raised Jesus from the dead and seated Him at His right hand in heaven to rule over everything here on earth and in all eternity. God saved us by His grace, raised us up with Christ, and seated us with Him in the heavenly realms. Satan has been given his place already. He now resides under the feet of Christ, below His authority and below the authority of Christ's body, the church, which includes all believers.

I believe in Christ; therefore, I have Jesus' power and authority over Satan, sin, and death. Through the Holy Spirit living in me, I have the same power that raised Jesus from the dead. If you believe in Jesus, so do you. Exercise authority and stand firm in the finished work of Christ, believing the truth. Resist the devil, and don't be trapped by His snares of falsehood and temptation. Don't give him more power than God has given Him. You are alive in Christ! Live in the grace and authority of Christ so you may carry out the work God prepared in advance for you to do. (See Ephesians 2:4-10.)

Through inner healing prayer and conversations, God spoke sincere, truthful words to me, healing the deepest wounds of my heart. He exposed my childhood belief in the deceit Satan had fabricated in my heart and mind. He gave me a new identity: "I am a child of God; He wants me and loves me." Not only did my thinking change, but Jesus Christ Himself engraved it on my heart. He showed me the truth, and the truth set me free. God loves me more than I will ever comprehend, and He wanted me, even before He created the world.

I am a child of God; He wants me, and He loves me.

When you have some time to yourself, seek God and ask Him to replace the lies you believe in your heart with His perfect truth. Ask for His protection from your enemy. Listen to His voice of truth in your thoughts. Confirm what you hear by finding God's truth in His Word, the Bible. Spend time developing a deeper intimacy with Him. Ask Him what He wants to teach you. Absorb the healing He gives! Then find it in your heart to forgive the one(s) who hurt you.

Reward #2 - Find Freedom in Forgiveness

In my mid-thirties, I learned from my sister that my mother tried to terminate her pregnancy with me. This new information devastated me. I needed to talk to my mom to find out why she went to this extreme. However, I couldn't discuss it with her because she had died of cancer after my twenty-first birthday. I was left with the burden of sorting it out on my own. I didn't want this news to set me back emotionally when Jesus had brought me so far in the healing journey. Fortunately, I could trade Him the heavy weight of my burden for a lighter load. The emotional healing He had already given afforded me the necessary foundation for processing this upsetting information more quickly and easily, to the degree that is feasible in Christ alone. I couldn't dwell on this new discovery. I needed to get rid of it as soon as possible.

After experiencing God's restoration of my broken heart, it was time for me to extend forgiveness to the one who hurt me—my mother. My mom was a wonderful woman, so I know deep down she would not have tried to get rid of me in the womb if Satan had not tricked her into feeling helpless and hopeless. I imagine the news she had become pregnant at forty while using birth control shocked and disappointed her. She found herself in a situation she did not want to be in and despaired. She herself may have been depressed. The enemy deceived my mom with lies; she believed ideas that did not hold true. She did not consider that God had planned her pregnancy. She didn't know her part in the bigger picture.

STEP 6 – ENJOY THE REWARDS

I feel blessed God chose her to be my mom. I know eventually she did love me very much. I do not tell my story to dishonor her in any way. I tell it because it's God's story of His healing and transformation in my life. His plan and purpose for creating me was to use me to bring glory to Him by sharing His message of redeeming grace and His passion for spiritual intimacy with His children. If God had not allowed me to experience the depths of this story, I would never have needed Him or made the time to listen to His voice. In hindsight, I am now thankful God permitted me to endure these trials to help me grow up spiritually. I'm forever changed by God. He deserves all the glory, honor, and praise.

Still, I felt a need to address my mom about her actions when she carried me in her womb. I needed release from the emotions surrounding my knowledge of her attempts to miscarry or terminate the pregnancy. Since I couldn't speak with her in person, I decided to write a letter to express my heart to her. It allowed me to release my feelings and empowered me to let go of my anger, blame, and disappointment. I could forgive her even though she had already passed away. Once more I was set free from things I tightly held. Forgiving is not necessarily a feeling; sometimes it's a choice.

An unforgiving heart is a roadblock to God's construction work in you. With the strength and power of the Holy Spirit inside you, find it in your heart to forgive the ones who have hurt you. If you are holding on to some emotion—anger, guilt, shame, or an unforgiving spirit—regarding someone who is alive or deceased, I recommend you write a letter to him or her. Then let it go and let God do a redeeming work in your life. No longer do I carry the burden of an unforgiving spirit. I have been released from my yoke of bondage. You, too, will find freedom in forgiving. Forgive others as God in Christ has also forgiven you. (See Colossians 3:13) Freedom feels fantastic! When the roadblock comes down, your ears will be open to encouraging words directly from the mouth of God.

Reward #3 - Enjoy the Encouragement

Who doesn't want to hear an encouraging word from God? We all desire His unfailing love. There's a God-shaped hole inside each of us only He can fill. He designed it that way. Sensing unmet needs, we search for things that will satisfy us: love, relationships, food, alcohol, drugs, material possessions, independence, wealth, success, and recognition. When we acquire and achieve those things, however, we remain empty and unsatisfied. We continue to yearn for the one thing that will bring us long-lasting happiness and fulfillment.

God created human beings with a hunger and thirst only He can satisfy. He wants us to be dependent on Him for everything. He wants to be in close relationship with each of us. Only God can love us perfectly and completely. No human being can match the love He has for you and for me. Nothing can satisfy our longings except the One who placed those desires in our hearts. Food, alcohol, and drugs bring temporary satisfaction until the effects have worn off, leaving us craving more. Material possessions and wealth provide the illusion of happiness for a time. However, some of the richest people in the world experience poverty in their spirits. Money and personal belongings do not bring lasting joy. Success and fame are achieved through long hours of hard work and dedication, often leaving little time for relationships and an unbearable loneliness.

As stated earlier, God used my depressive episodes to get my attention. He wanted me to experience more of Him, so He could fill me up with His love, encouragement, and companionship. I exude gratefulness as I remember how God worked through my Christian mentor to fascinate me with a new and exciting relationship with Jesus. I received spiritual guidance on how to get close to God by listening to His voice. It was the best thing He could have done for me. It sparked my interest in pursuing a deeper, more intimate relationship with my Lord.

In my depressed and dejected state of mind, I had a very low opinion of myself. I felt unattractive, unappreciated, unwanted, and unloved. Each time I met with God, He rebuilt my soul with kind, encouraging words. In our daily conversations, God told me what I meant to Him. He informed me I'm made in His image and He doesn't make mistakes. He stated I'm beautiful on the outside and the inside. He reminded me He wanted me and loved me before He created the world. He showed me how precious I am to Him and how much He enjoys spending time with me. He demonstrated my value as His creation, and He revealed my worth as His heir. He delivered me from my enemy, Satan. He liberated me from captivity.

He refined me and equipped me to carry out His purpose for creating me. He helped me see myself through His eyes.

Below are a few of my Quiet Time journal entries. I hope you find God's words encouraging for yourself, too. In all my journal entries, my thoughts are written in regular text and God's words to me are *italicized.*

Journal Entry on 10/09/2004

Lord, I read through yesterday's journal. I see You want to be involved in everything I do, even the small stuff. Lord, would You help me remember to let You in and check with You on everything throughout the day? Please speak to me today. I would love to hear from You.

O My daughter, I love you. I love to listen to you share your heart with Me. I want to hear from you all day long. I want you to share every emotion, every struggle with Me. I want you to breathe a prayer to Me all day long. Pray without ceasing. Let Me in on everything. Nothing is too small for Me. I want to know all the details. When you seek Me and trust in Me this way, you will experience the kind of intimacy your heart desires. I am your Father, your friend, the lover of your soul. I desire to dance every step of your life with you, but I will not force you to spend time with Me. I wait for you to desire it too and find your way to Me. Then I'll welcome you with open arms, embrace you, and lead you through the dance of your life. I'm always with you—not just in the morning. You can talk to Me all day long. I expectantly wait to hear from you. I love you, and I long to spend time with you. Give Me a chance. You won't believe what you will feel. It will be better than anything you could imagine. I'll be right here waiting for you. I love you.

I love You too, Lord. I want what You want. Please help me get there.

Journal Entry on 10/13/2004

Lord, I keep hearing from You that You want to be even more personal with me. What else do You want me to learn?

You are getting it all. Here's how your day should go. Every thought you have, check it out with Me. I'll help you discern My thoughts from yours and your enemy's. Every emotion you have throughout the day, check it out with Me. I'll help

STEP 6 – ENJOY THE REWARDS

you understand each one. Whether it's a genuine emotion that comes from a fully alive heart or a reaction used as a defense mechanism to protect a wounded spot in your heart, I'll help you sort through it all, and you'll become more emotionally healthy in the process. All day, seek Me before you let any words flow from your mouth. Let Me check your words and replace the ones that should be replaced with Mine. That way, you'll never use too many words or too few; you'll use just the right words to give a praise, to minister to a hurt, to convict a heart, to instruct a child, to discipline a child, to speak the truth in love, to be My instrument. You can spend many hours every day, all day, doing something you think is right. But that may not be the best use of your time. Let Me direct your actions, every one. Make sure you aren't just spinning your wheels. Satan would love to have you spend time doing things, even good things, that seem right to do, rather than seeking Me and doing exactly what I want you to do. Before you take one step throughout your day, ask Me. Before you spend time going in a direction, make sure it's where I want you to go. Let Me lead. I told you I'll be with you every step of the way, but I prefer to lead. Will you let Me lead?

Journal Entry on 10/23/2004

Dear Lord, will You please sit with me this morning? Father, may I rest in You today? I had a very busy week and I just need to relax in Your arms. Will You quiet me with Your love? Lord, my mind is racing off in a few different directions; would You please help me focus on You? Help me to be still and know You are God. Lord, fill me with Your peace. Would You please speak to me and help me to listen and hear Your message correctly?

My daughter, you are My delight. I love this time we spend together in the morning. We don't have an agenda. We can just communicate about whatever the day brings. I remain with you. You don't have to face anything alone. I know all your thoughts, fears, joys, disappointments. I can help you through each one. I anxiously wait for you to seek Me. I long to be everything to you. I want to be involved in every detail, plan, conversation, action, and emotion you have. Please seek Me more often. When you are afraid, call on Me. When you are angry, vent to Me. When you are lonely, invite Me in. When you are happy, let's celebrate. When you are sad, let Me comfort you. When you are anxious, let Me calm you. When you are nervous, I'll quiet you with My love. When you are tired, I'll be your strength. When you are broken, I'll heal you. Please call on Me more often. Please invite Me to participate in everything you do. I am with you always.

Before and during my depression, my fire for life had burned down to a mere ember. Meeting with God daily and listening to His voice ignited a new fire of passion in me for knowing the *living* God who dwells in me. When you recognize and hear God's voice on a regular basis, it brings new meaning to an otherwise dull, lifeless existence. Let God be the fuel for your heart's fire. Listen to what He wants to say to you. As Paul stated in 2 Thessalonians 2:16, let God's words to you "encourage your hearts and strengthen you in every good deed and word." Make time to meet with God daily. Enjoy the encouragement, and let God love you. Discover the deeper, long-lasting joy that comes from being obedient to the Holy Spirit's instruction.

Reward #4 - Follow the Instruction

God speaks to His people not only to encourage us, but also to instruct us in life. Psalm 32:8 says, "I will instruct you and teach you in the way you should go; I will counsel you and watch over you." He shares His wisdom, His commands, and His teachings throughout the Bible. For example, read Proverbs 2 to catch a glimpse of the benefits of seeking God's wisdom. Also, Jesus sums up the greatest commandment in Matthew 22:37-38 when He says, "'Love the Lord your God with all your heart and with all your soul and with all your mind.' This is the first and greatest commandment. And the second is like it: 'Love your neighbor as yourself.'" These are instructions to live by.

Seeking God's wisdom by listening to His voice and then following through on His instructions leads to a life of intimacy, peace, and joy with the Lord. When we tune our ears to God's voice, quite often we hear or feel the Holy Spirit prompting us to do something important. Just as a parent instructs a child and expects obedience, God expects us to obey when He speaks to us. When we do not obey His voice, we miss out on some great opportunities to experience the plans He made for our lives, including the benefits of lasting joy, indescribable peace, and abundant blessing—the kind of full life Christ came to give us.

Proverbs 8:10-11 says, "Choose My instruction instead of silver, knowledge rather than choice gold, for wisdom is more precious than rubies, and nothing you desire can compare with her." In this verse, God compares His instruction to precious metals and reveals a worth far greater than silver or gold. Nothing you desire or money can buy surpasses the rich wisdom imparted in God's instructions.

In John 14:23, Jesus shared an insight on how to experience intimacy with God: "Jesus replied, 'If anyone loves me, he will obey My teaching. My Father will love him, and We will come to him and make Our home with him.'" When we love Jesus, we will obey His teaching. When we obey His teaching, God loves us and makes His home with us. We learn and grow in intimacy with God. Jesus didn't leave us guessing how to get close to God. This verse came in the context of Jesus promising to send the Holy Spirit to live with us. God dwells with those who love and obey Him. He doesn't just visit us from time to time; He makes His home in us forever. Jesus modeled His love for God by being obedient to His Father's instructions, even unto death on the cross. It's not enough to listen to God's voice. We also must obey.

Sometimes the Holy Spirit wakes us up in the middle of the night or early morning to instruct us. If you wake up and can't get back to sleep, get out of bed and have a conversation with God. We can hear Him anywhere and anytime we listen. God's Word in Joel 2:28-29 confirms the Spirit of the Lord speaks to men and women through dreams and visions: "And afterward, I will pour out My Spirit on all people. Your sons and daughters will prophesy, your old men will dream dreams, your young men will see visions. Even on My servants, both men and women, I will pour out My Spirit in those days."

I know people today who hear from the Lord in their dreams. I do not hear from Him this way, but I understand why some do. When we are at rest and do not have the distractions of the day, God speaks to us in the quiet of the night. Job 33:14-18 says,

> For God does speak—now one way, now another—though man may not perceive it. In a dream, in a vision of the night, when deep sleep falls on men, as they slumber in their beds, He may speak in their ears and terrify them with warnings, to turn man from wrongdoing and keep him from pride, to preserve his soul from the pit, his life from perishing by the sword.

Listen to the instructions and warnings from God as He speaks to you while you sleep. Many times, the middle of the night is the only time our hearts and minds are still enough to hear Him. Consider what He might be saying to you in your dreams, visions of the night, or sleeplessness.

In Acts 1:1-2, Paul reminds Theophilus that before God took Jesus up to heaven, Christ *gave instructions through the Holy Spirit* to the apostles He had chosen. He sent the gift of the Holy Spirit to us so He could continue to teach us and give us instructions after He returned to the side of God the Father. When the Spirit of God instructs us, He does not allow us to forget about what He wants us to do. In my experience, the Spirit does not let me ignore His instructions. He persists until I obey. Here is one example:

Many years ago, after I had experienced this deeper intimacy with Christ, the Holy Spirit prompted me to be baptized by full immersion. This happened years before our church held full-immersion baptisms in the sanctuary on Sunday mornings, but I talked to my pastor about it. He willingly offered to perform the baptism in the swimming pool of a member who lived behind the church; he had done it once or twice before.

I didn't know why God called me to do this. My parents had me baptized as an infant, so my husband and I didn't understand why I needed to be baptized again. Because it did not represent an ordinary practice for my church at the time, I put it off. I tried to forget about it, but the Holy Spirit didn't let me. He first prompted me at the beginning of the summer, and throughout the following months, He continued to remind me He wanted me to be baptized.

As the end of summer drew near and we skidded into the end of pool season in Michigan, the Spirit impressed on me if I didn't do it now, I would have to wait another ten months. I talked about it again with my husband; I discussed it with my pastor; and I had many conversations with God about it. God exercised tremendous patience with me as I learned to discern His voice and verify His instructions. I needed more confirmation, and I needed to feel the peace of God in my spirit about it. The journal entry below reflects one of the many conversations I had with God. Note that my thoughts are in regular type, while God's thoughts are *italicized* in all my journal entries.

Journal Entry on 8/14/04

Lord, I love You. Thank You for prompting me in my spirit to be baptized by full immersion. I want to be obedient to You, but I feel resistance from within and from others. Lord, please confirm for me You want me to do this.

My Spirit is in you. Nothing can take that away. When the enemy tries to diminish what I have set up for you, do not let him win. You take your instruction from Me. I have given you this baptism opportunity. Do not allow the enemy or His helpers to deter you from this assignment. I want you to be baptized for Me as a sign and seal of your full devotion to Me. Let no one take it from you. It is My design for your life. It is part of your sanctification process. It is a covenant between you and Me. You are making Me Lord of your life, and I remain in you. I will never leave you. I immerse you fully in My living water. I baptize you with My Spirit. You are Mine.

For weeks, I fretted and wrestled with being obedient to the directions of the voice I heard in my head. When I read my journal entries again, I realize how immature in my faith I acted. Still new at listening to God's voice back then, I wanted to make sure I heard Him correctly. Satan battled hard for my obedience to him rather than God. The devil nearly succeeded, and I almost missed my chance to obey God's instructions. Don't be as thick-headed as I acted. Again, God exercised extreme patience with me as I learned to trust in Him and His voice. Be sure to confirm His commands until you feel peace about them, but don't allow Satan to have such a great influence on your decision-making and your timetable that you miss the opportunity to obey the prompting of God's Spirit.

Obedience to God's instructions always produces immense joy in my spirit. This incredible joy is reflected in this post-baptism journal entry:

STEP 6 – ENJOY THE REWARDS

Journal Entry on 08/28/2004

Lord, I'm so full of You and Your glory right now. I can hardly contain myself. Praise You, Lord! You are awesome and mighty and holy and great! You are my God and King. I praise Your name! You are worthy of my praise. You reign on high and You reign in me. My heart burns inside me from Your Spirit on fire within me. I glow with Your beauty. I have never been more radiant. Your image in me has been revealed, and I cannot run and hide any longer. You radiate from my face. I will praise You all day and all night. You fill me with Your glory. Your Spirit reigns within me. My heart flips somersaults on the inside because I feel so happy. When I practice obedience, You fill me with joy and it feels fantastic. Again You have allowed me this time of pure rejoicing and protected me from the blows of Satan, the deceiver. Don't allow him to make this less than it is. You reign, Lord! All people in attendance there tonight know You reign in me. My soul dances on the inside. I dance before You, Lord. My spirit rejoices inside me. My heart leaps with joy. You have made me fully alive in You, Lord. Thanks for calling me out. Thanks for waking me up. Thanks for using me and helping me become more like Jesus. You are the Lord of my dance. You lead me in the dance of my life; I rest in

Your arms of love. I delight in You and You delight in me. I cannot wipe this smile off my face. I am pleased by You and You are pleased with me.

Thanks for the joy that fills my heart right now. I wish it would never end. I fear hitting the trenches again tomorrow and facing Satan's attacks. I will not let him win, however. I sold my heart to the devil for nothing, but You paid a tremendous price for me. You came to rescue me so I could experience life to the fullest. You are my abundant joy. Forever, I will praise Your name, O Lord. You are the Most High God. You are awesome in power and "Mighty" is Your name. O Lamb of God, my Savior, my Friend, I love You, Lord. I never want this night to end. Your joy and love abound inside me. You are my Lord for now and forever. You reign in me. My heart is Yours. My soul is Yours. My mind is Yours. My strength is Yours. You alone are worthy to be my Lord. You alone are worthy of all my praise. Bless You, Lord. You are righteous and holy. All glory and honor and praise belong to You. I cannot say enough. You are God, and who am I? I am Yours! I am Yours! I am Yours!

After the baptism, I experienced almost as many days of overwhelming joy as I had of overshadowing doubt before the experience. When you are obedient to God's instructions and the prompting of the Holy Spirit, you will experience incomparable joy just as Jesus' disciples did in Acts 13:52: "And the disciples were filled with joy and with the Holy Spirit." Don't put off doing the will of God. When you hear God's voice and instructions, don't wait months to carry them out. Confirm what you hear, and then do it! When we're obedient to the Holy Spirit's promptings, we'll experience a greater joy lasting longer than any happiness we might receive from the things of this world. In Luke 11:28, Jesus says, "Blessed rather are those who hear the word of God and obey it."

Listen to God's instructions, "and the peace of God, which transcends all understanding, will guard your hearts and your minds in Christ Jesus" (Philippians 4:7). When listening to God doesn't bring you peace, however, it might be because the Holy Spirit is convicting you of sin.

Reward #5 - Consider the Conviction

One of our responsibilities as Christians is to change our old ways and obey the Holy Spirit's leading as He empowers us to become more Christ-like. This process is called sanctification. To be sanctified means to be holy, or set apart. Though we live in the world, we are strangers to it. We should act differently than our non-Christian friends do. Through the work of Christ on the cross, we have been consecrated and made righteous in Him. Our old sinful ways have died with Christ, and now we can lead a new life of righteousness in the resurrected Christ. As Christians, we should appear different to the world. We are made righteous in Christ, and we should choose to live accordingly, so the world may know we belong to God. Being a new creation is achieved, in part, when the Holy Spirit convicts us of a sin and encourages us to repent and change our ways. When we live as Jesus Christ did, it pleases God, and it provides a witness to a watching world. 2 Corinthians 5:17-21 says,

> Therefore, if anyone is in Christ, he is a new creation; the old has gone, the new has come! All this is from God, who reconciled us to Himself through Christ and gave us the ministry of

> reconciliation: that God was reconciling the world to Himself in Christ, not counting men's sins against them. And He has committed to us the message of reconciliation. We are therefore Christ's ambassadors, as though God were making His appeal through us. We implore you on Christ's behalf: Be reconciled to God. God made Him who had no sin to be sin for us, so that in Him we might become the righteousness of God.

Our sin separates us from God because He hides His face from wickedness. He sent His own Son, Jesus, to be our sacrificial lamb. Jesus Christ died on the cross to pay the penalty for our sin, so we could be reconciled to God. Jesus made us righteous and holy so we could enjoy a relationship with the righteous and holy God. Now He desires that we would set ourselves apart from the world. He wants us to lead lives that stand out from the way the rest of the world operates. He doesn't expect us to do this on our own, in our own power. He gives us the Holy Spirit, who convicts us of our sin and holds us to a life of righteousness.

All human beings have been given a moral conscience to know right from wrong. The problem with a human moral conscience is it's molded by each individual's experiences and life circumstances—which are not always true and pure in God's economy. This conscience is often derailed or overridden by our selfish, sinful flesh. In His saving grace, God gives believers a spiritual conscience—the Holy Spirit—who helps us discern right from wrong in His eyes. He convicts us of sin and empowers us to overcome the flesh and change our ways. "But he who unites himself with the Lord is one with Him in spirit" (1 Corinthians 6:17). We are directed to submit our spirit to the leading of God's Spirit within us.

In order to lead a God-pleasing life, we must read His Word to know what He expects of us. The Bible is very clear on what is sinful and what is righteous in God's eyes. When we obey Him and yield ourselves to the leading of His Spirit, He recalibrates our moral conscience to recognize sin, and then He helps us steer clear of it. When we do sin, He convicts us. The Spirit encourages us to make choices that will please God. He reminds us of what we know from God's written Word, convicts us of our sin, and empowers us to live a life of righteousness. In order to be led by the Holy Spirit, we must tune our ears inward to the broadcast frequency of the living God inside us. As Jesus said before His death,

"But I tell you the truth: It is for your good that I am going away. Unless I go away, the Counselor will not come to you; but if I go, I will send Him to you. When He comes, *He will convict the world* of guilt in regard to sin and righteousness and judgment: in regard to sin, because men do not believe in me; in regard to righteousness, because I am going to the Father, where you can see me no longer; and in regard to judgment, because the prince of this world now stands condemned." (John 16:7-11, emphasis mine)

Jesus provided the way to reconciliation with God, and then He provided the way to live a consecrated life by the power of the Holy Spirit. Jesus reunited us with God and gave us access to His power, so we may lead a life set apart for Him. It's up to us to choose. We can lead a life of sin in the flesh or righteousness in the Spirit. If we choose righteousness, you can be sure the Spirit convicts us when we sin.

It's important to understand the difference between conviction and condemnation. The Holy Spirit *convicts us* we are guilty of sin so we can confess it and ask God for His forgiveness. In contrast, the devil *condemns us* and causes us to wallow in guilt and shame. The Holy Spirit says, "You *did* a bad thing," while our enemy Satan says, "*You* are a bad person." The Holy Spirit encourages or prompts us to confess our sin; Satan accuses our person, attacks our identity, demeans our self-worth, blames us, and charges us for our sin.

Listen to the words Paul wrote in Romans 8:1-17 about how to live a life in the Spirit:

> Therefore, there is now *no condemnation* for those who are in Christ Jesus, because through Christ Jesus *the law of the Spirit of life set me free* from the law of sin and death. For what the law was powerless to do in that it was weakened by the sinful nature, God did by sending His own Son in the likeness of sinful man to be a sin offering. And so He condemned sin in sinful man, in order that the righteous requirements of the law might be fully met in us, *who do not live according to the sinful nature but according to the Spirit.*
>
> Those who live according to the sinful nature have their minds set on what that nature desires; but *those who live in accordance with the Spirit have their minds set on what the Spirit desires.* The mind of sinful man is death, but the *mind controlled by the Spirit is life and peace*; the sinful mind is hostile to God. It does not submit to God's law, nor can it do so. Those controlled by the sinful nature cannot please God.
>
> *You, however, are controlled not by the sinful nature but by the Spirit, if the Spirit of God lives in you.* And if anyone does not have the Spirit of Christ, he does not belong to Christ. But if Christ is in you, your body is dead because of sin, yet *your spirit is alive* because of righteousness. And if *the Spirit of Him who raised Jesus from the dead is living in you*, He

who raised Christ from the dead will also *give life to your mortal bodies through His Spirit, who lives in you.*

Therefore, brothers, we have an obligation—but it is not to the sinful nature, to live according to it. For if you live according to the sinful nature, you will die; *but if by the Spirit you put to death the misdeeds of the body, you will live, because those who are led by the Spirit of God are sons of God.* For you did not receive a spirit that makes you a slave again to fear, but *you received the Spirit of sonship.* And by Him we cry, "Abba, Father." The *Spirit Himself testifies with our spirit that we are God's children.* Now if we are children, *then we are heirs—heirs of God and co-heirs with Christ*, if indeed we share in His sufferings in order that we may also share in His glory. (Emphasis mine)

When we make a conscious effort to listen to the Spirit of God within us, we hold the keys to life and peace. We must allow our minds to be controlled by Him. Paul says we are obligated to be *led* by the Spirit. Does Satan continue to hold you in bondage and defeat? Or does God's Spirit guide you into freedom, victory, and peace?

Jesus already fought and won against our enemy. If we share in His sufferings, we may also share in His glory. We can claim victory over our struggles, addictions, temptations, and obsessions because Jesus won the war and put His Spirit in charge of us. When we obey Him and submit ourselves to His leadership, we will experience life and peace. Consider the conviction of the Holy Spirit when you are reminded of your sin and prompted to repent.

I fight a constant fleshly battle with the sin of gluttony. I find myself indulging in foods I don't need. I have a deadly attraction to carbohydrates and sweets, especially chocolate. I love to bake and prepare delicious foods, and then I love to eat them—until they are gone. I do not exercise much self-control with food. I don't stop at one or two bites; I have to eat the entire serving or batch. Not only do I not exercise self-control, but I do not physically exercise much, either. Too much rich food and too little exercise is a lethal combination of worldly behaviors.

Self-control is a fruit of the Spirit. (See Galatians 5:22-23.) The Holy Spirit is ready and willing to help me fight this battle. All I need to do is call on Him and He's got this—He'll strengthen me with self-control so I may deny myself the pleasures of unhealthy food and larger portions than my body needs. Ashamedly, I admit too often, I simply ignore the voice of the Spirit telling me not to partake in the food I'm about to eat. I know if I submit myself to the voice of the Spirit and draw on His power from within me, I could resist the temptation to indulge in the food that entices me. But at times I make a conscious choice to willingly give in to the flesh. I'm not proud of this. The Spirit is willing to help me, but my flesh is weak. I would be successful in denying myself this gratification with food if only I would listen to the conviction of the Holy Spirit, tap into His power, and *live in the Spirit*, obeying Him.

Sometimes I choose to comfort myself with food, rather than allowing the Holy Spirit, my Comforter, to console me and ease my emotional pain. It's much like an alcoholic might comfort himself with alcoholic spirits over the Spirit of life. When I give in to the lure of food, I disappoint myself, feeling guilty for my poor choices. I can't tell you how many times my behavior has disappointed God when I allowed myself to be controlled by the flesh, rather than drawing on the power of the Spirit to resist temptation. The momentary pleasure and satisfaction I get from food are nothing in comparison to the long-lasting comfort, peace, and joy I would experience from being obedient to the Holy Spirit's leading. Moreover, my sin results in being overweight and unhealthy, which hinders me in fulfilling God's plan for my life.

The Holy Spirit speaks to us to keep us from sin and wrongdoing. Are you listening? You may not be able to relate to the sin of gluttony. What's your crutch? What's your downfall? Do you have an addiction? Has the Holy Spirit convicted you of a behavior you need to change? Jesus Christ was fully man, yet He remained pure, without sin, a spotless lamb. It's by the power of the Holy Spirit, the same Spirit we have access to, that Jesus lived a life without sin. His strong love and passion for the Father gave Him the dedicated fervor to resist all temptation and choose obedience. Just as Jesus spent time alone with God to receive His guidance and direction, He also drew on the power of God's Spirit within Him to overcome the will of the flesh.

Regularly tuning in to the voice of God, the Holy Spirit within, accomplishes a giant step in the process of sanctification. If we are going to become more like Christ, we must not only listen to the voice of God, we must obey it. When you feel the Spirit prompting you to do or not do something, don't ignore Him. When you feel a tug on your heart to carry out an assignment from God, no matter how big or small, be quick to comply. When you know the Spirit of God has spoken instructions to you, act upon them as soon as possible. When a human spirit yields to the control of the Holy Spirit, the result is life and peace. Choose to *live in the Spirit* and be at peace with God. Listen to His voice, and consider the conviction. Is there a sin you need to confess or turn from? What is the Holy Spirit asking you to do or not do? What behavior do you need to change? What action have you been prompted to take?

The other type of conviction that the Holy Spirit prompts us with is the strong confidence and certainty we have in the saving grace of God. We are called to be His witnesses to this grace. 1 Thessalonians 1:4-5 says, "Brothers loved by God, we know that He has chosen you, because our gospel came to you not simply with words, but also with power, with the Holy Spirit and with deep conviction." There are times when the Holy Spirit convicts us to attest to the goodness of God and the gospel of good news. Let me encourage you, as I should also be encouraged, to take advantage of every opportunity the Holy Spirit offers us to be a witness of the gospel.

For many, many years, I acted timidly in expressing my faith. I did not possess the confidence necessary to give a good verbal witness to anyone. However, the healing, love, and encouragement God showed me through my depression fortified my foundation of faith and my trust in Him, to the point where I could not keep quiet about how good He had been to me. I know He used my struggles to bring me into a more intimate relationship with Himself, and He wants me to share this experience with everyone. God wants to use my story to inspire others to be devoted to listening to His voice and cultivating a deeper intimacy and stronger relationship with Him.

As God strengthened my trust in Him, He equipped me with the confidence I needed to express my faith in word and in action. Only by the power of the Holy Spirit of God did I find a new certainty in my faith, enough to be able to speak to groups without buckling at the knees and suffering anxiety attacks. Although I remain nervous enough to stay humble, knowing I could not speak in public from my own strength, the Holy Spirit gives me the confidence I need to share my story and obey God by completing the assignments He gives me. It is no credit to me, but all glory goes to the One who makes my heart His dwelling place. When the Spirit gives you a deep conviction to be a witness for Christ, He also equips you with great power where none existed before, so you can do what He wants you to do. Listen to the call of Christ on your heart. What are you being called to do? Acting on the conviction of the Holy Spirit is the wisest way to live.

Reward #6 - Savor the Wisdom

Appreciate and enjoy God's wisdom. Cherish it more than everything. As believers in Christ Jesus, we have access to all the treasures of His wisdom and knowledge. The Spirit of God, who lives within us, knows the things of God and makes them known to us. His wisdom is more precious than rubies. Nothing compares to it. According to the two verses that follow, God's wisdom is a priceless treasure:

> My purpose is that they may be encouraged in heart and united in love, so that they may have the full riches of complete understanding, in order that they may know the mystery of God, namely, Christ, in whom are hidden all the treasures of wisdom and knowledge. (Colossians 2:2-3)
>
> I have not departed from the commands of His lips; I have treasured the words of His mouth more than my daily bread. (Job 23:12)

How do we gain complete understanding of God's wisdom? How does the Holy Spirit make the things of God known to us? Let's take another look at what Jesus said in John 16.

> I have much more to say to you, more than you can now bear. But when He, the Spirit of truth, comes, *He will guide you* into all truth. He will not speak on His own; *He will speak* only what He hears, and *He will tell you* what is yet to come. He will bring glory to Me by *taking from what is Mine and making it known to you*. All that belongs to the Father is Mine. That is why I said the Spirit will take from what is Mine and make it known to you. (John 16:12-15, emphasis mine)

Through Jesus Christ, we have access to all that belongs to God. His gift of the Holy Spirit dwelling in our hearts is the most priceless treasure! Without the Spirit of God living within us, we might not be able to hear His voice or have instant, direct access to His wisdom as He relays it to us.

Jesus did not say the Spirit would speak only to a select few. Jesus said He *"will guide you"* and *"will speak"* and *"will tell you"* and *"make it known to you"* (emphasis mine). As children of God who have accepted Jesus Christ as our Savior, we all have access to His wisdom through the Spirit of God within us. If you believe in

Jesus Christ, the Spirit *will speak* the wisdom of God to *you*. Are you listening?

"A voice came from the cloud, saying, 'This is My Son, whom I have chosen; listen to Him'" (Luke 9:35). God the Father told us to listen to His Son. Jesus is in God and God is in Jesus, so however we stack it up, we just need to listen to God's voice and savor the wisdom. Savor means "to enjoy, to delight in, to value, and to appreciate."[2] Are you enjoying the wisdom God has for you? Do you delight in Him and value the knowledge He gives you? Do you appreciate the access to all that belongs to God the Father through His Son, Jesus Christ, and His gift of the Holy Spirit dwelling in you?

If you better understood the value of hearing God's voice and receiving wisdom from Him, would you make the time to listen more often? Proverbs 2:1-6 says,

> My son, if you accept my words and store up my commands within you, turning your ear to wisdom and applying your heart to understanding, and if you call out for insight and cry aloud for understanding, and if you look for it as for silver and search for it as for hidden treasure, then you will understand the fear of the Lord and find the knowledge of God. For the

Lord gives wisdom, and from His mouth come knowledge and understanding.

Through the Holy Spirit dwelling in us, we have access to God's wisdom directly from the mouth of God Himself. Isn't that the best news you've ever heard? Have you tried turning your ear to the voice of God to receive His wisdom? Have you applied your heart to understanding through the voice of His Spirit within you? Do you desire to have God's wisdom so much you are willing to "look for it as for silver and search for it as for hidden treasure" (Proverbs 2:4)? Will you put forth the effort to garner the wisdom of God by listening to His voice before everything else? Proverbs 2:6 says, "From His mouth come knowledge and understanding." Why don't we seek God by listening to His voice more often? Why don't we go to God first to gain His wisdom for everything we say and do?

When I first started listening to God's voice, I brought many, many problems and situations before Him and asked for His wisdom in dealing with each challenge. He gave me answers time after time. His wisdom came through the guidance of His Spirit in the form of

STEP 6 – ENJOY THE REWARDS

instructions, insights, and reminders. Here is an excerpt from my journal in which God instructs me from His wealth of wisdom how to have true delight. When we practice the wisdom of God, following His informed insights, we will experience lasting joy.

Journal Entry on 09/13/2004

Lord, how can I have an unending supply of Your true joy?

You have My joy at your disposal all the time. Joy is the fruit of the Holy Spirit, whom I sent to live inside you when you accepted Me as your Savior and Lord. You can tap into that joy 24/7. It is a gift from Me, and it is freely given, just like My grace. You have to practice being joyful. You will receive an abundance of joy each time you yield in obedience to Me. This kind of joy will make your smile beam from ear to ear. This joy will make you want to dance before Me. This joy will well up inside you and burst forth like a fountain or a rushing waterfall. This joy will bring tears to your eyes and warmth to your heart. This joy is different than the happiness you get from the world, happiness that's dependent upon your circumstances, others around you, and your relationships. But My joy is yours all the time. My joy is in you, and your joy is made complete. My joy is your strength.

True joy is very inviting. It makes others wonder what you have that they do not. Be joyful at all times. Rejoice in the good times and in the bad. Again, I say, "Rejoice!"

Here is an excerpt from my devotional book **Manna for Today: Bread from Heaven for Each Day**. This is a message that Jesus, who is the embodiment of God's wisdom, spoke to me.

Wisdom of God[3]

It is because of Him that you are in Christ Jesus, who has become for us wisdom from God—that is, our righteousness, holiness and redemption. (1 Corinthians 1:30)

I am wisdom from God. The wisdom of the wise has been destroyed. The wisdom of the world has been made foolishness. In the wisdom and power of God, I have come to save the world. You are not considered wise by the world's standards. Your belief in Me may give you the label of the foolish one in this world, but I have overcome the world. The foolish will shame the wise. Do not speak of the wisdom of this age, but of God's secret wisdom and power.

STEP 6 – ENJOY THE REWARDS

You have the Spirit of wisdom within you. The Spirit of God, who dwells within you, knows the thoughts of God and makes them known to you. You will, therefore, speak words not of human wisdom, but of God's wisdom taught to you by His Spirit. Because the Spirit of God lives within you, you have the mind of Christ. You have spiritual wisdom and discernment because the Spirit of God is in you. You may know and understand the things of God because you have been given the Spirit of God.

God has made foolish the wisdom of the world. You were born of the world and taught the wisdom of the world. Now, you are born again with the Spirit of the Lord; and therefore, possess the wisdom of God. God's wisdom is supreme. Get wisdom and understanding though it may cost you all you have.

Wisdom will protect you and guide you on straight paths. I am the wisdom of God. I will protect you and guide you. My Spirit lives within you. You have access to the wisdom of God at all times. Listen to My words with all your heart; I give you sound learning. Do not forsake My teaching. Keep My commands, and live in the wisdom that God has given you.

God waits for us to seek Him in everything we do. He longs to impart His wisdom for our everyday challenges. His Spirit will guide us in His wisdom, if only we ask. Many times, the Spirit of God guides you even when you don't ask. Are you listening to the still, small voice of God within you? Will you search for God's wisdom as you would search for hidden treasure? Will you make it a priority to meet with God and listen to His insight? When you do, you will savor the wisdom of God and enjoy the fruit of His peace.

Reward #7 - Delight in the Peace

By the time I reached my mid-thirties, I had created a busy life for myself. I had everything I wanted: a husband, a home, a job, a girl, a boy, friends, a dog, God, a church, a ministry, and much more. Why did I feel so empty? I controlled my life—or did my life control me? My life resulted in exactly what I had made of it, not what God had planned. My life was good, but it was not God's best for me. My life felt full, but I remained hollow. My *whole* life had left me with a *hole* in my heart. Our definition of a full life is different than God's. The life I had created quickly spun out of control and into depression. I was in *pieces* and had no *peace* within.

God met me at the bottom of my pit of depression. He stretched out His hand to me. I took hold, and He pulled me up. He set me down on His firm foundation and began the rebuilding process in me. As I learned to trust God more every day, I turned over new areas of my life to Him. When I turned over complete control to God, He rearranged major things in my crazy, busy life to give me the peace He wanted me to enjoy.

After many months of meeting with God on a daily basis to listen to His voice—absorb His healing, find freedom in forgiving, enjoy His encouragement, follow His instruction, consider His conviction, and savor His wisdom—I could now delight in His peace. God had rebuilt my demolished soul through the work of His Holy Spirit inside me. He gave me a newfound confidence in Christ and in myself as a child of God. He gave me a renewed relationship with the Father. He gave me a stronger, more vibrant faith and a passion for serving my Savior. He gave me more spiritual knowledge and a better understanding of the Holy Spirit and His role of transforming me into a new creation.

Let me be clear. Life did not get a lot easier, but it did become more peaceful as I gave over control to God. That statement seems contradictory. Losing control should not produce peace in one's spirit, but the things of God are not as they seem. He does not operate as the world does. When I gave up control and surrendered to the will and plans of God, He lifted a burden from me. As I consulted with Him in all areas of my life, big and small, I turned from being a people-pleaser into being a God-pleaser. I didn't care as much about what people thought anymore; I concerned myself with what God thought. I did not have to please everyone; I had to please *the One*. I tried not to spread myself thin going in too many different directions. I focused my attention in one direction—up.

It took many months for God to rearrange my life in order to give me the kind of peace He wanted me to experience by trusting fully in Him. I had obligations I needed to fulfill and positions I had to find replacements for. I had to change the way I operated in my home among my family. As God freed up my time by releasing me from a few responsibilities, I became more available for Him to use in His work.

God started me out with small challenges to equip me and prepare me for greater ones. He gave me confidence for the assignments I received. He gave me fortitude and determination. He gave me a passion for His people and His message. Doing God's work generated a much greater reward than anything I might take on myself. With obedience come peace and joy. It just feels right. It feels good to live with a heart at peace, rather than in turmoil. That is not to say God's work is easy to accomplish, but the reward is worth the effort. Not only did God free up my time, but He answered many years of prayers by freeing up my husband's time too. I now spend more time with my husband than I ever dreamed of or asked for. Never give up on placing your requests before the Lord. He answers all prayers in His perfect time, sometimes in greater ways than you ever thought possible.

As I faithfully met with God every morning, our relationship deepened immensely. He did a great deal of intense work with me on discovering, processing, and healing my emotional wounds. I shed many tears along the path to healing. The rough and rocky emotional journey had to be traveled to get to a better place—a place of freedom, peace, and rest.

While shopping in a mountain gift shop in the beautiful state of Colorado, I found a sterling silver ring with the word *PEACE* engraved on the top. I purchased it to wear every day to remind myself of who God is, what He has done for me, and the place He has brought me—*PEACE*. Jesus, the Prince of Peace, has engraved His name on my heart. The ring symbolizes a fitting memento for the peak of my healing journey.

One of the first observations my Christian mentor made about me all those years ago was that I did not have much peace in my life. It was a very smart—and true—observation. I experienced a full life, yet I did not know what peace-full felt like. Some people do not experience a *full* life according to worldly standards but have a life *full* of peace and contentment because they rely on intimate communication with God through the Holy Spirit, rather than depending on things and circumstances. The *full* life Jesus Christ came to give us equals a life *full* of His peace when we are in tune

STEP 6 – ENJOY THE REWARDS

with the voice and Spirit of God, not based on material possessions, human relationships, or excellent conditions.

Jesus stood at my door and knocked. I answered and let Him in. I spent time with Him and listened to His voice. I pursued Him, drew near to Him, and remained in Him. The outcome has been a deeper, more intimate relationship with my Savior. The lasting effect is a life full of His peace. I now know the peace of God, even in the midst of life's challenges.

Get close to God by being in touch with God's Holy Spirit inside you. Tap into the power of the Prince of Peace, who lives in your heart. Listen to God's voice and experience a life full of His perfect peace. Psalm 85:8 says, "I will listen to what God the Lord will say; He promises peace to His people, His saints—but let them not return to folly." Listening to God's voice enables us to delight in His peace. The peace of God is more precious than diamonds, silver, or gold. Enjoying all the rewards of listening to God makes me want to share this excellent practice with the world.

STEP 6 - SELF-REFLECTION:

1. What do you desire God's healing for in your life?

2. God has forgiven you. Whom do you need to forgive?

3. What do you need God's encouragement in?

4. What instructions has God recently given you? Will you obey them?

5. What is the Holy Spirit convicting you of right now?

6. How will you seek God's wisdom?

7. Do you desire the peace of God? What steps will you take to attain it?

7-DAY CHALLENGE:

Spend the next seven days asking God to gift you with the seven rewards covered in this chapter. On the first day, seek God for healing in one area of your life. On the second day, ask God to help you forgive one who has offended you. On the third day, seek God's encouragement where you need it most. On day four, ask God for

STEP 6 – ENJOY THE REWARDS

help obeying His instructions. On day five, pay attention to the conviction of the Holy Spirit. Is He prompting you to confess and change your ways, or inspiring you to witness to someone you influence? Day six offers you the opportunity to seek God's wisdom for a situation you face. On day seven, bask in the peace and presence of your Savior. Meditate on your favorite Bible verse about peace and picture yourself in a beautiful nature setting, enjoying a relaxing moment with Jesus. Whatever you ask for in Jesus' name is yours!

STEP 7

SHARE THE GOOD NEWS

The practice of "show and tell" in elementary schools is much more than filling time in the classroom. This tradition helps the student learn to articulate her thoughts, feelings, and opinions to her peers. She realizes her conviction about a particular item or topic. She expresses her passion about the item she shares. Sometimes classmates ask questions about the item, which deepens the certainty of the one showing and furthers the audience's knowledge and understanding. This custom makes students aware of things they may otherwise never see or hear about.

I followed Christ more than twenty years before I learned the art of listening to God's voice. I knew God spoke to a few people,

STEP 7 – SHARE THE GOOD NEWS

but I didn't believe He would speak to me, a minor player in the big scheme of things. If early in my walk of faith a more experienced Christian had practiced "show and tell" with me, I could have been listening to God's voice for many, many more years. When you know something really great—when you have access to a priceless piece of art—you show and tell others about it. You show them what it means to you and tell them how to achieve it for themselves.

Enable others to enjoy the treasure you already enjoy. Tell people they can hear the voice of God. Show them the art of listening to Him. This is my prayer for you: "I pray that you may be active in sharing your faith, so that you will have a full understanding of every good thing we have in Christ" (Philemon 6).

As we wrap up our time together, I have a request: Please do a better job than I have done as a wife and mother in sharing your relationship with Jesus Christ and your ability to hear God's voice with your spouse, your children, and their children. Satan wants nothing more than for us to keep this priceless treasure to ourselves. When I started hearing God's voice, my enemy, the devil, took notice. Satan stood on full alert and wanted to stifle me before I became a threat to his work. He introduced new lies to me, and, naively, I believed them. I crawled into my prison cell once again when I believed in the opponent's deceit. He cunningly ran these crafty thoughts through my mind: *You hear God speak? Really? People will think you are crazy. You'd better keep this one to yourself. No one will believe you. They will think you are foolish. They will lock you up and throw away the key. Your husband won't believe you. He'll think you are unstable—after all, you are depressed and taking medication. Your children won't understand. Don't even try to share this with them.*

Do you feel as unhappy about this as I do? Have you ever had similar thoughts? I allowed Satan, the destroyer, to shame me right into silence. I wasn't crazy but naïve—not fully aware and alert to my spiritual opponent. I was not knowledgeable and experienced in the ways of the devil. I kept this wonderful news of hearing God's voice all to myself. I shared it only with my mentor, who heard God's voice too.

I played right into Satan's hand. If he could keep me silent about listening to God's voice, he had me exactly where he wanted me. Nobody would know about it. Nobody would hear the good news. Nobody would be encouraged to listen to God speak. Nobody would believe they could hear the voice of God in their thoughts. The enemy had me believing I lived on an island, all alone. Satan convinced me that many believers do not hear God's voice, and I'd be crazy to say I do. Therefore, I supposed I should not tell anyone I practice listening to God and I recognize His voice.

As soon as I became wise to Satan's deceitful ways, I began the battle of breaking free. King Jesus came to my rescue again. The Holy Spirit used Scripture to educate me about the devil's ways. He instilled confidence in me because Christ has already won the battle against my enemy. Christ has set me free. Paul tells us in Galatians 5:1, "It is for freedom that Christ has set us free. Stand firm, then, and do not let yourselves be burdened again by a yoke of slavery." I remain free now to show others what God has done for me and to tell them how to listen to His voice.

I learned to pray the Armor of God, from Ephesians 6:10-18, to protect myself. He showed me how to rebuke the devil and stand strong in the victorious name of Jesus Christ. He gave me the sword of the Spirit, which is the Word of God, as my weapon of choice. Not only did I have a new passion for Christ, I had a new hatred toward the devil. I would stand firm in the finished work of Christ. By the power of the Holy Spirit, in the name of Jesus Christ, I would win this battle in my mind. I would be excited to "show and tell" the world how to practice the art of listening to God.

In my weakness, Jesus Christ strengthened me for battle. He protected me from my enemy and equipped me to stand victoriously in authority over Satan. Jesus prepared me to carry out my purpose in God's greater plan. I'm nobody special, except that I'm a child of God. He had me in mind before He created the world. He wanted me and loved me before He set the stars in the sky. He uses the common, the lowly, and the unlikely ones to carry out His plans. I represent the common, lowly, and unlikely. I am an ordinary woman who can hear from an extraordinary God. He used my story and prepared me to share it to bring His people into closer relationship with Himself. God has called me to deliver a message to His people. This is the message God wants me to share with you:

> *God loves you more than you will ever comprehend.*
> *He wants to have an intimate relationship with you.*

STEP 7 – SHARE THE GOOD NEWS

He speaks to you, and He wants you to listen. He has more to say than a "yes" or "no" to your requests. He wants you to put Him first in your life by spending time with Him daily, listening to His voice, and carrying out His will.

Spending time in relationship with Jesus Christ to develop the art of listening to God is the best thing I've ever done in my life. Well, it's a close second to the decision I made to accept Jesus Christ as my Savior. Listening to God and hearing His voice is priceless—a valuable art form. Will you search for it as for silver? Building intimacy with Jesus Christ is building spiritual wealth in the kingdom of God, here on earth and in heaven. Will you pursue it as you would hunt for gold? The wisdom of God is more precious than rubies. Will you seek it around every corner?

Right now, I implore you to reclaim any power you have relinquished to the enemy and empower your family, your friends, your children, and your children's children by passing on this precious gift of knowledge to them. Do not fear; be strong and courageous. Tell those you influence to put God first—to spend time with Him and listen to His voice. Train them in the ways of God, and then train them in the ways of Satan, their enemy. Educate them and equip them to stand firm and claim Christ's victory in their own battles.

Demonstrate how to know God better by saturating yourself in His Word and meditating on it day and night. Encourage your children to do the same. Place them into God's care and protection, so they may develop a greater intimacy with and trust in the One who created them. Teach them how to listen to His voice by modeling this behavior yourself and by sharing your own experiences with them. In the words of Charles Stanley, children will "do what we do before they do what we say."[4] So be sure you are practicing what you are preaching, and then instruct the next generation and beyond, using the four T's:

1. *Tell* them to put God first by making time for Him, making Him a priority in their lives.

2. *Train* them to know God better by reading His Word and meditating on it day and night.

3. *Trust* them to deepen their relationship with Jesus Christ by spending time with Him in the person of the Holy Spirit and yielding their own spirit to His.

4. ***Teach*** them to "listen" to the voice of God within themselves—listen and obey.

When you believe in God and accept Jesus as your Savior, He sends His Holy Spirit to live in your heart. The *living* God dwells in you! Look within your own spirit, and tune in to the Spirit of God. Jesus promised the Spirit of Truth would speak to you and make the things of God known to you. You have access to everything that belongs to God—to His very mind and thoughts. God and Jesus speak to you through the Holy Spirit, who speaks to you in your thoughts. Listening to God's voice within you is one of the keys to experiencing an abundant life—the full life Jesus Christ came to give you. When you can hear the voice of God, you have everything you need; you are filled with all the fullness of Christ. When you hear God speak to you, it will change your life forever.

Now believe it and do it! Go and listen to the voice of God! God will bless you richly as you seek to know Him more intimately.

Respond to God's voice in the words of the boy, Samuel: "Speak, for Your servant is listening" (1 Samuel 3:10). May God bless you with His presence and His word as you seek to know Him better every day. Know and cherish God's voice within you!

STEP 7 - SELF-REFLECTION:

1. What priceless treasure of truth about God could you share with others?

2. What are you passionate about? What lights you on fire for the Lord?

3. How could you get your message out of your heart and into the world? How can you show it? How can you tell it?

4. In what ways could you start sharing this valuable gift of knowledge with your family, your friends, your co-workers, your children, and your children's children?

5. Think hard about this: Do Satan's lies in your thoughts keep you from sharing the message God wants you to communicate to others?

STEP 7 – SHARE THE GOOD NEWS

6. What is your battle plan to break free from Satan's captivity and claim your victory in Jesus' name? Remember God is for you; who can be against you?

7. List the names of seven people you want to share your message with. Make or seize an opportunity over the next seven weeks to accomplish this goal.

7-DAY CHALLENGE:

Ask God to present you with an opportunity to share Him and His love with one of the people you listed above. Ask for the insight to see the opening and the courage to follow through. Pray for grace mercy, and truth as you communicate the message of God's love for His people and His desire for close relationship with His children. Then, cherish the joy that fills your heart as God rewards your obedience.

CONCLUSION

Hearing God's voice is my greatest joy in life. Years ago, in my quest to hear it, I discovered I had to search no farther than my own heart and mind. Sometimes, I think we expect to experience God's voice as Moses did—from the burning bush. When in reality, God most often chooses to whisper to us in our thoughts. We will perceive His voice best when we give Him our undivided attention. Open your mind and heart to whatever way God wishes to speak to you—in your thoughts, through Scripture, through a friend, in the words of a song or book, in your dreams and visions, or any other way He chooses. The truth is **God does still speak**—Are you listening? Give it a try. Your life will never be the same again!

Thank you for spending this time with me and allowing me to share with you what I have learned about listening to God's voice. An ordinary person can hear from an extraordinary God. Are you ordinary? If so, you can hear from Him too.

I would love to assist you in your endeavor to hear God's voice on a daily basis. What are your biggest challenges in listening to God? Please email them to me at sindynagel612@aol.com

My devotional book, *Manna for Today: Bread from Heaven for Each Day*, will inspire you and give you the necessary jumpstart for listening to God's voice on a daily basis. *Manna for Today* is written in God's voice. Use it as a springboard into a quiet time with God, where you may develop your own way of listening to His voice. Whatever you do, do it with all your heart!

In the love and service of Jesus Christ,

Sindy Nagel

Author/Speaker/Blogger

Thank You!

As a special "Thank you" gift to you, we are offering a free color .JPG file you can print off and keep in your quiet time journal, so you may refer to it as you meet with God to listen to His voice.

7 Simple Steps to Hearing God's Voice - Infographic

Grab your free color infographic on the "**Welcome!**" page at:

www.sindynagel.com

Also watch for Sindy's forthcoming books in the

Hearing God's Voice Series:

7 Roadblocks to Hearing God Speak

7 Times to Listen to God

7 Places to Listen to God

7 Ways to Listen to God

7 Roles of the Holy Spirit

7 Rewards of Hearing God's Voice

Follow Sindy's Blog

www.sindynagel.com

Follow Sindy on Facebook and Twitter

https://www.facebook.com/pages/Sindy-Nagel-Author/324224121010277

www.twitter.com/SindyNagel

See Sindy's Author Page on Amazon

http://www.amazon.com/Sindy-Nagel/e/B00BAJKYEM

Purchase Sindy's Other Books

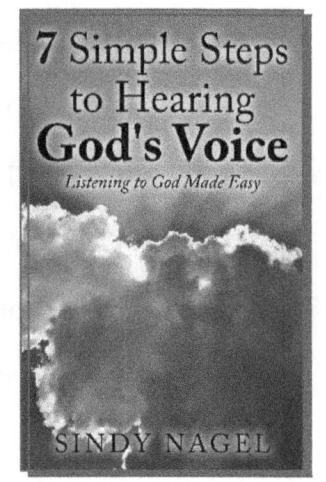

7 Simple Steps to Hearing God's Voice

ISBN 978-0-9969934-0-1 (Paperback)

ISBN 978-0-9969934-7-0 (eBook)

ISBN 978-0-9969934-3-2 (Audio)

Manna for Today

ISBN: 978-1-4497-6704-4 (Paperback)

ISBN: 978-1-4497-6705-1 (Hardcover)

ISBN: 978-1-4497-6703-7 (eBook)

Publisher: Westbow Press (A Division of Thomas Nelson)

[1] Thesaurus in Microsoft Office Word2013, s.v. "practice," accessed April 18, 2014.

[2] Thesaurus in Microsoft Office Word 2013, s.v. "savor," April 14, 2014.

[3] Sindy Nagel, "Wisdom of God" in *Manna for Today: Bread from Heaven for Each Day* (Bloomington, IN: WestBow Press 2012), 139.

[4] Dr. Charles Stanley, In Touch Ministries with Dr. Charles Stanley, sermon titled, "Leaving a Godly Inheritance," aired on Lifetime television on May 11, 2014.